The author gratefully acknowl
Comunn Gaidhealach in the ti

To Kim –

St Oran's Chapel
19 September 2002

and of course to Joyce and Lindsay
and to Richard

Iona –
a guide to the Island of Druids, Saints and Dreams

with illustrations by Judith Long

Published by Kayelle Productions Ltd.
www.kayelle.co.uk

Printed in Great Britain by Aldine Print Ltd., Malvern

A copy of the CIP entry for this book is available from the British Library

ISBN: 0-9547640-0-5

Iona

a guide to the island of druids, saints and dreams

Simon Andrew Stirling

a guide to the island
of Druids,
Saints and Dreams

Iona

what's in a name?

The origins of the name 'Iona' are obscure. While it is true that Columba, the name of Iona's most renowned resident, signifies '**dove**' in Latin, and Iona ('Jona') means '**dove**' in Hebrew, this appears to be more a happy accident than the actual derivation of the name. The dove makes its appearance in the contemporary sculpture situated in the grassy quadrangle of the abbey cloisters. The symbol derives from the ancient idea that the soul turns into a dove at the moment of death, and in many older cultures the dove is a feminine symbol of wisdom, peace and the soul.

In the Book of Genesis, Noah sends forth first a raven and then a dove from the Ark. The first time, "the dove found no rest for the sole of her foot" and returned. Seven days later, "the dove came in to him in the evening; and, lo, in her mouth was an olive leaf, pluckt off". After another seven days, the dove flew again, and was gone. Both the raven and the dove have a significance in the history of Iona.

In the third chapter of the St Matthew's gospel, Jesus is baptized in the River Jordan by John the Baptist:

"And Jesus, when he was baptized, went up straightway out of the water: and, lo, the heavens were opened unto him, and he saw the Spirit of God descending like a dove, and lighting upon him".

In Gaelic, Jesus is '**Iosa**'.

Jonah ('Iona') also means dove. The story of Jonah is that of a man who tried to flee from the presence of the Lord by taking ship: "But the Lord sent out a great wind into the sea, and there was a mighty tempest in the sea, so that the ship was like to be broken." The mariners drew lots to decide who was the cause of the storm, and Jonah confessed. Cast overboard, Jonah was swallowed by a "great fish" – "And Jonah was in the belly of the fish three days and three nights."

In the belly of the whale, Jonah prays: "The waters compassed me about, even to the soul: the depth closed me round about, the weeds were wrapped about my head. I went down to the bottoms of the mountains: the earth with her bars was about me for ever: yet hast thou brought up my life from corruption, O Lord my God." (Jonah, Chapter Two, verses 5 and 6.)

Returning to the Book of Matthew, we read the words of Jesus to the Pharisees: "An evil and adulterous generation seeketh after a sign; and there shall no sign be given to it, but the sign of the prophet Jonas:

"For as Jonas was three days and three nights in the whale's belly; so shall the Son of Man be three days and three nights in the heart of the earth." (Matthew, Chapter Twelve, verses 39 and 40).

What is that sign of the prophet Jonas, if not the dove of rebirth and tranquillity.

In the eighteenth century it was suggested that Iona was originally Ì Eòin: the **Island of St. John**. There is an Eilean Eoin – 'John's Island' – facing the abbey across the Sound of Iona: two lumps of Caledonian Granite and a thin strand of sand that shelter Uamh nam Marbh – the 'Cave of the Dead' – from the sea.

The Christian church turned the old Midsummer Festival into the Feast of St. John, at the opposite pole of the year to the Nativity, and given that pagan shrines, gods and festivals were adopted and adapted by the early church, we can assume that a hard-hitting Christian saint was needed to sanctify a popular pagan ceremony. Similarly, it would be a fair assumption that an island associated with pagan rituals would require dedication to the Baptist to establish its Christian credentials.

Eòin is the Gaelic plural of eun, meaning 'bird'. No visitor to the island could doubt that a suitable name would be I-eòin, '**Island of Birds**'.

The Gaelic name for Iona is, simply, '**I**'.

Legend states that when Columba and his companions were sailing towards Iona, one of them suddenly cried out: "Sút ì!" ("There she is!"). Columba exclaimed:

Mar sud bithe I, goir thear II ... "Then so be it, and let her be called 'I'." The vowel is pronounced 'ee'. Columba chanted: Dochím hÍ, bendacht ar gach súil docí -

"I see Iona!
A blessing on each eye that sees it!
He who does a good for others here
Will find his own redoubled many-fold!"

'I' is the Gaelic third person feminine pronoun, meaning 'she', 'her' or 'it'. It is also the eighth letter of the Gaelic alphabet, in which all letters are styled after trees, and 'i' relates to 'iubhar' – the yew.

Adomnán, writing at the end of the seventh century, refers to Ioua insula – the Isle of Ioua, or Iouan Island. Early names for the island included Hii and Ie, which could be adapted from the Norse 'ey' except that they generally appear before the Norse influence was reckoned to be that great. It is most likely that like the fellow names for Iona – Io and Eo – they derive from the Middle Irish 'iwos' and the Old Irish 'eó', signifying the stem or trunk of a tree, in particular the yew. This would make Ioua 'the yewy isle' or the '**Island of Yews**'. It would have been a trifling scribal error to turn a 'u' into an 'n'; it might even have been a deliberate act, thus turning the Yewy Isle into the Dove, Columba's Isle: I-Chaluim Chille. We might note in passing that 'Eo' means '**salmon**' in Irish, as in Eo Feasa, the mythical Salmon of Wisdom.

The yew was one of the Five Magical Trees of Ireland, alongside the oak, rowan, elder and hawthorn. It was the cultus arborum of the Druids – the "firm, strong god" – a symbol of the soul's immortality, and its magical uses included spells for raising the dead. The evergreen longevity of the yew tree (most churchyards in Britain harbour at least one; some have lived more than 2,000 years) not only preserved the dead but offered long life to the living. Tradition states that wands of white yew were used at the inauguration of kings and chieftains.

The yew is, of course, entirely poisonous, and was considered a protection against fire in the Hebrides. A Highlander would clutch a yew sprig when hurling threats against his enemies: the yew would render his challenge inaudible to his opponents, thus retaining for the Highlander the all-important element of surprise.

An Irish source even refers to Iona as Innis Dhruidhnean – **Island of the Druids** – or Innis Dhruidnechean – which better translates as '**Island of the Craftsmen**'. Caution is necessary when writing of the druids, and some authorities insist that Iona's associations with the druids were born of eighteenth century romanticism. However, it would be wrong entirely to discount the likelihood of druidic practice on Iona before the coming of Columba's monks.

Around 1850, the suggestion was put forward that Iona might derive from Ì shona, sometimes referred to as **Island of the Saints**. However, the Gaelic for saint is naomh, as in ionad naomh – a holy place or sanctuary – and there is an Eilean nam Naoimh, or Island of the Saints, in the Firth of Lorne, where St. Brendan of Clonfert settled twenty-one years before Columba arrived at Iona. The adjective 'sona' denotes lucky, fortunate or happy. Thus we get Ì shona, the Happy Isle, or **Isle of the Blest**. In the classical world, the Isles of the Blest were believed to lie in the western sea.

In 1792, the Reverend Dugal Campbell translated Iona as the **Island of the Waves**, from I-thonn.

Earlier, in the ninth century, the German monk Walahfrid Strabo wrote:-

Insula Pictorum quaedam monstratur in oris,
Fluctivago suspensa salo, cognominis Eo
Qua sanctus domini requiescit carne Columba.

"On the Pictish coast is an isle of the sea,
Floating amidst the waves, Eo is its name,
Where rests the body of the Lord's saint, Columba."

By that point, Iona was becoming widely known as Ì Coluimb Chille – the **Island of the Church of Columba**, or the Isle of Columba of the Church. It is this that William Shakespeare preserves in 'Macbeth' some eight centuries later:-

ROSS: Where is Duncan's body?
MACDUFF: Carried to Colme-kill,
The sacred storehouse of his predecessors,
And guardian of their bones.
Act II, Scene 4)

Or, later still, in the words of William Wordsworth:

Homeward we turn. Isle of Columba's Cell,
Where Christian piety's soul-cheering spark
(Kindled from Heaven between the light and dark
Of time) shone like the morning star, farewell!

For nigh on a thousand years, she was Icolmkill or I Chaluim-chille, but before that she was 'I', as in the familiar verse attributed to Columba:

An I mo chridhe, I mo ghràidh
An àite guth mhanach bidh géum ba;
Ach mu'n thig an saoghal gu crích,
Bithidh I mar a bha.

"In Iona my heart, Iona my love,
The voices of monks shall become the lowing of cattle;
But before the world come to its end,
Iona shall be as she was."

For the island is '**She**' ... **The** Island.

The Holy Isle of the Western Sea.

"In the Isle of Dreams
God shall yet fulfil Himself anew"

Gaelic prophecy

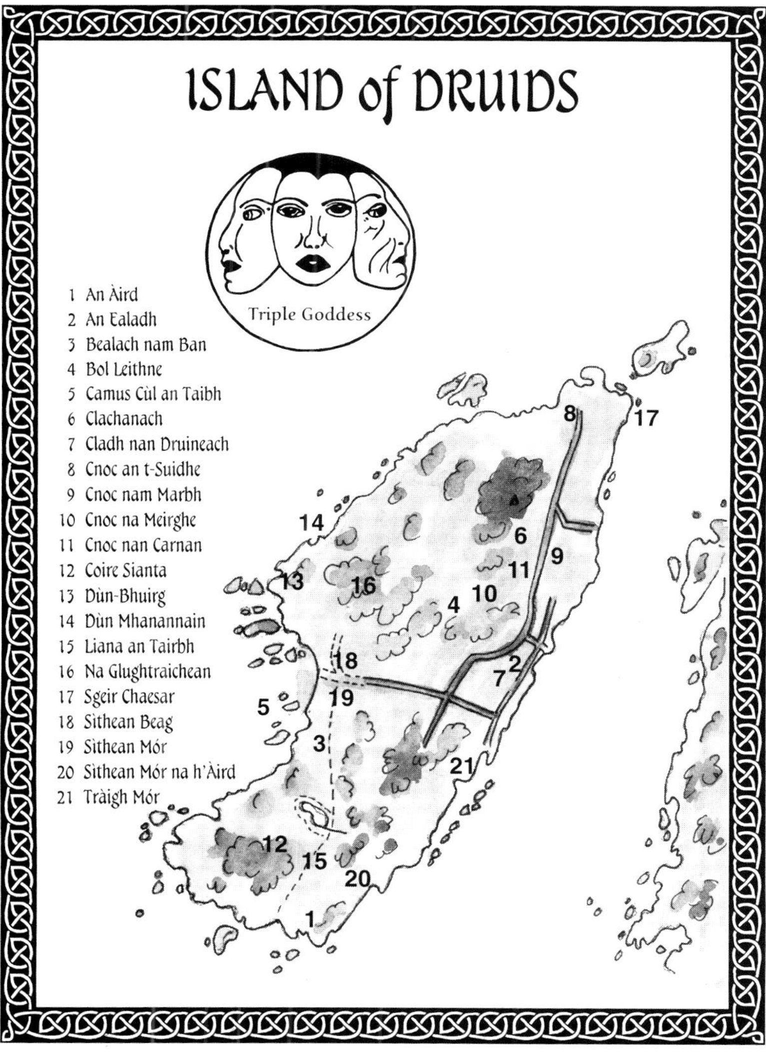
ISLAND of DRUIDS
Triple Goddess
1 An Àird
2 An Ealadh
3 Bealach nam Ban
4 Bol Leithne
5 Camus Cùl an Taibh
6 Clachanach
7 Cladh nan Druineach
8 Cnoc an t-Suidhe
9 Cnoc nam Marbh
10 Cnoc na Meirghe
11 Cnoc nan Carnan
12 Coire Sianta
13 Dùn-Bhuirg
14 Dùn Mhanannain
15 Liana an Tairbh
16 Na Glughtraichean
17 Sgeir Chaesar
18 Sìthean Beag
19 Sìthean Mór
20 Sìthean Mór na h'Àird
21 Tràigh Mór

IONA

Island of Druids

Island of Druids

I nam ban bòidheach
- "Iona of the beautiful women"
(Gaelic proverb published by Alexander Nicholson, 1881)

To outside eyes, Iona is simply a tiny island – three miles long and a mile and a half wide – nestling like a leaf in the ocean off the south-west tip of Mull. To those who peer a little closer, she becomes something else: a spiritual touchstone and powerhouse, the resort of pilgrims for centuries. Iona has been referred to as the 'thin isle', since the veil between this world and the Otherworld is readily penetrable on her resplendent shores.

Iona is chiefly composed of the world's oldest rocks. The Lewisian Gneisses that make up the bulk of the island were amongst the first to be created on the earth's crust, making her considerably older than her much larger volcanic neighbour.

If Iona was one of the first landmasses to rise above the primeval ocean, there is an ancient prophecy that claims she will be one of the last to sink:

Seachd bliadhna roimh'n bhràth,
Thig muir thar Eirinn ré aon tràth,
'S thar Ile ghuirm ghlais,
Ach snàmhaidh I Choluim chléirich.

"Seven years before the Last Day,
The sea shall come over Ireland in one season,
And over blue-green Islay,
But swim will the Isle of Columba the cleric."

The extreme age of Iona's rock, and the belief that she shall outlast other islands, no doubt contributed to the desire of chiefs and kings to be buried there. It might also have attracted those early ministers whom custom has come to know as the Druids.

The traveller who reaches Iona via the mainland port of Oban and the Caledonian-MacBrayne ferry to Craignure will have crossed what the poet Keats described as "a most wretched walk of 37 miles across Mull". Less than three miles to the south of Duart Castle is Grass Point, below which we find Port nam Marbh: the 'Port of the Dead'. A line of standing stones stretched across the Ross of Mull from Grass Point to Fionnphort, suggesting that the 'pilgrim route' to Iona Ferry is of very great antiquity indeed.

Fionnphort ('White Port') is a sandy bay facing Iona across a mile of sea and surrounded by the distinctive pink rocks upon which Columba is supposed to have seen angels beckoning to him, although 'it was not yet his time'. Immediately before entering Fionnphort, the visitor passes reedy Loch Poit na h-Ì – perhaps a place for depositing votive offerings prior to the sea crossing. The loch, with its chapel facing the road and a standing stone placed directly across the road from the loch, adjoins the tiny hamlet of Pottie, which surely derives from the same meaning: 'Pot of Iona'.

Immediately to the north of Fionnphort lies a strip of sand, shielded from the sea by Eilean Eoin, where we find the 'Cave of the Dead'. It seems probable that when rough weather prevented a sailing across the Sound of Iona, the corpse being carried to the sacred isle might have been sheltered here by an Cois na Mara. Further still to the north, beyond the Red Port and Eilean nam Ban, lies the 'Black Isle of the Coffin'.

Island of the Women

The ferry heading west-north-west from Fionnphort to Iona passes on her right-hand side the tiny Frenchman's Isle, beyond which is Eilean nam Ban: 'Island of the Women'. In his 1928 guide to 'Iona Past and Present', Alexander Ritchie suggests that 'women' refers to 'the nuns'.

According to legend, Columba banished women and cattle from Iona:

> Far am bi bó bidh bean,
> 'S far am bi bean bidh mallachadh.
>
> "Where there is a cow there will be a woman,
> And where there is a woman there will be cursing."

The assumption followed that Eilean nam Ban was where the wives or partners of labourers working on Iona were housed.

The injunction against cows is peculiar, given the fact that the monastery kept its own herd. Adomnán writes – tellingly – of Columba driving out a devil that was hiding in a pail of milk. The channel of water that separates the Island of the Women from Mull is called Poll Tairbh – the pit, or hole, or possibly nostril of the Bull.

Just to the south of Fionnphort is the 'Port of the White Cow', and the peninsula known as Eilean nam Bó, or 'Island of the Cow', stands close to Fidden and faces the southern-most point of Iona.

On Iona itself, we find at the north-eastern extremity Sgeir nam Mart, which means the Cow's Rock, although 'mart' tends to signify a cow due for slaughter. On the north-west facing coast we find Carraig an Daimh – 'Rock of the Ox, or Oxen' – adjoining Sloc na Bó Duibhe, the 'Gully of the Blacker Cow'. Cnoc nam Bó, or 'Hill of the Cow', overlooks Sligeanach on the east coast, and the 'Meadow of the Bull' – **Liana an Tairbh** – lies between the 'Big Hill of the Strangers' and **An Àird**, on the approach to the 'Big Fairy Mound of the Height'.

Given that in all other respects Columba's attitude towards women was benevolent, could his alleged banishment of women and cows from Iona be related to his efforts to overcome paganism? To the Celt, the cow had an especial importance.

Boand, the Irish goddess who gave her name to the River Boyne, was 'She of the White Cows'. Also in Ireland, the Tarbfeis or 'Bull Sleep' was a method for divining the next king by sacrificing a bull, washing in the broth and eating its flesh, and then 'sleeping on the question'. We read in The Dream of Rhonabwy in the Welsh 'mabinogion' of a yellow ox-skin on a platform, "and lucky the man who was privileged to sleep on that." The Irish Druid, Mac Roth, called for his "skin of a hornless, dark-grey bull and white-speckled bird headdress" and rose up "into the air and heavens" to do battle against an opposing Druid. The Pictish Druid Drustane, during a war waged alongside the Irish against the British, caused a pit to be filled with the milk of 150 white-faced cows into which wounded warriors could be immersed to emerge fully cured.

Martin Martin, in his 'Description of the Western Isles' (1695), describes a method of divination known as taghairm, which means 'an echo', or divination through the use of demons. One form of this method involved the seer, who was frequently chosen by lot, wrapping himself in the hide of a newly-slaughtered bull and lying down by some spirit-haunted place to await the message from the sìthean or from spirits rising from the sea.

According to Lewis Spence ('The Magical Arts in Celtic Britain'), "Tradition speaks of 'Isles of Women' in both Ireland and Scotland, where Druidesses dwelt apart from their husbands at certain seasons."

Both Strabo and Pomponius Mela refer to an island off the coast of Gaul. This was Sena – or Ile de Sein – near Brest, the "abode of priestesses holy in perpetual virginity, and nine in number." Strabo refers to the priestesses as "possessed of Dionysus", who was also known as 'Io'. They were believed to hold extraordinary powers, including control of the winds and seas, shape-shifting, healing and prophecy. Once a year, they celebrated a ritual which involved re-roofing their temple in the space of a single day. If one of them – apparently chosen in advance – happened to stumble, she was torn apart by her fellows: an ecstatic ritual that must have suggested the Dionysus reference since it recalls the behaviour of the Maenads and Agaüe, who tore her son Pentheus to pieces in her Dionysiac delirium.

The island of Anglesey – Ynys Môn in Welsh, Mona to the Romans – was attacked by Suetonius Paulinus in the spring of the year 60 because it housed a prominent and influential Druidic college. Tacitus provides a description of what greeted the legionaries: "On the beach ... a packed mass of men and arms, with women slipping between the ranks, like Furies, wearing death-black robes and with their hair dishevelled they wielded their torches". Tacitus also describes a circle of Druids who struck awe into the battle-hardened Romans, paralysing them until their general incited them not to be cowed by "a band of females and fanatics". Mona was razed, the sacred groves of the Druids cut down, and probably in response to this horrific treatment of the Celtic holy men Boudicca of the Iceni rose up against the Roman occupiers, destroying Colchester, London and St. Albans before meeting her untimely end at Mancetter.

Thus we can identify two islands of the Celtic world – Sena and Mona – that Roman sources tell us were used by Druidesses or women associated with Druids. Plutarch, who died in 120, referred to an island near Britain where there was "an order of Magi, reputed to be holy by the people." The Rev. W.L. Alexander insisted that a Druidic college existed in 'the isle of the Druids' in the Western Isles until Columba arrived in 563. If the Druids of Gaul preferred wands of oak, the Irish Druids considered the yew, hawthorn and rowan sacred, hence – perhaps – their fascination with the 'yewy isle'. Indeed, Columba himself encountered 'Druids' on his arrival at Iona.

Bride

The first Christian saint to be associated with Iona was Brìde (pronounced: breed) who, as St Brigid, or Bridget of Kildare, is one of Ireland's patron saints. Born seven years before the death of St. Patrick (about 461) she died two years after the birth of Columba.

According to the legends, 'Bride of the Hebrides' was born into poverty, though of the same race as the princely Columba, and grew up in exile on the south-east slope of Dùn Ì. Only the

Arch-Druid knew of her background and, referring to an ancient prophecy, announced "Truly this child is an Immortal ...

"There shall be, it is said, a spotless maid born of a virgin of the ancient immemorial race in Innisfail. And when for the seventh time the sacred year has come, she will hold Eternity in her lap as a white flower. Her maiden breasts shall swell with milk for the Prince of the World. She shall give suck to the King of the Elements."

This Bride, described as a "golden, sparkling flame", became the foster-mother of Christ. A fine and colourful pre-Raphaelite canvas by John Duncan depicts the girl, with flowing tresses, transported by angels over the sea from Iona to Bethlehem to attend the birth of Jesus, where she wrapped the infant in her plaid, hand-woven on Iona.

Bride, or Brigid, was originally Brigantia, a goddess widely worshipped throughout Britain and Ireland. In Irish mythology she was the daughter of Anu, mother goddess of the Tuatha de Danaan, gods of Ireland who appear to have developed into faeries. As a goddess of knowledge, she was a favourite of the poets and bards, as well as being a goddess of fire – hence a connection with craft and smithwork – and fertility, giving her the status of patroness of midwives and women in labour. In her Christianized form her feast day is Candlemas, the beginning of February, a festival associated with the Purification of the Virgin. In the pagan calendar, this is Imbolc, sacred to the goddess in her maiden state, symbolic of new light and life appearing out of the harsh darkness of winter. Her festival is probably the origin of today's Valentine's Day.

At her shrine in Kildare ('Church of the Oak'), a sacred flame was tended by her maidens. A fence surrounded the shrine to prevent any man peeping at the sacred virgins. The legend, based around the English Midlands, of Lady Godiva, who rode naked through the streets of Coventry in protest against severe taxes levied on the peasantry, preserved elements of the Brigid or Brigantia rituals. The original "Peeping Tom" was blinded for gazing upon her as she passed covered only by her golden hair. At the forefront of her pageant marched "Old Brazen-face", a character wearing a bull's head mask and horns. Godiva herself was followed by a second Godiva figure, this one 'stained black', recalling the 'Black Annis' who was another version of the goddess Anu – a fertility goddess worshipped especially by women, and a name sometimes given to Brigantia. The goddess was known as the 'Two-Faced One', with one half of her face dark and ugly and the other half pale and beautiful. This is because the maiden form of the goddess (spring) inevitably transforms into her hag form, or 'cailleach', in winter. There is a Buaile nan Cailleach, or the 'Old Woman's Cattle-fold' heading into the southern end of the island, just beyond **Bealach nam Ban**, 'Pass of the Woman'. 'Cailleach' can also mean a 'veiled one', or 'a nun'.

Here we have an ancient goddess, associated with fire, fertility, poetry and healing, as well as cattle, adopted by the Christian church and identified with Iona.

Chuir Brìghd' a làmh sa bhobhla – 'Brigid put her hand (or handle) into the bowl' – states an old Gaelic proverb. This is thought to refer to St. Bride's miraculous ability to turn water into ale.

As late as the eighteenth century, it was the custom on the island to celebrate Maundy Thursday as Diardaoin a Brochain Mhóir: 'Thursday of the Great Porridge'. As the day began, a man waded into the sea and poured out an offering of gruel, chanting:

> "O God of the Sea,
> Put weed in the drawing wave
> To enrich the ground,
> To shower on us food."

The cauldron of inspiration and plenty was a magical item to the Celts, and developed into the Grail of Arthurian Romance. The Welsh bard Taliesin ('Shining Brow'), who flourished in Columba's century, describes the cauldron of the Welsh goddess Ceridwen as the 'Cauldron of the Five Trees', and elsewhere as 'the Cauldron of the ruler of the deep'. In some legends, it was a bath which rewarded the initiate with immortality but deprived him of speech. Taliesin tells us that the mystical brew in Ceridwen's sacred cauldron included berries, cresses, sea-foam, wort and vervain. Vervain was widely revered, not least by the Druids, and St. John's Wort was a particular favourite of Columba's. Similar cauldrons of mystery include the mixture of sea-water, salt, barley, laurel and flowers sacred to Ceres, the Roman fertility goddess. Did something of this magical gruel survive in the Maundy Thursday ritual?

What of the cauldron itself? Taliesin informs us that 'By the breath of nine maidens it is gently warmed', and that 'It will not boil the food of a coward not sworn'. They tend the cauldron in a quadrangular sanctuary in 'the island of the strong door', perhaps the island mentioned as Seon and identified by Lewis Spence as Ile de Sein, or Sena, where nine priestesses dwelt. Seun in Gaelic means a charm, especially one that could protect invisibility (the Old Irish is sén) and Seonaidh is 'Shony'.

Shony was a sea-god, believed to be of Norse origin. Fiona Macleod recorded the rhyme of a little girl, singing and playing by the waves on the shore of Iona:

> "Shanny, Shanny, Shanny,
> Catch my feet and tickle my toes!
> And if you can, Shanny, Shanny, Shanny,
> I'll go with you where no one knows!"

Shony wasn't necessarily a benevolent god of the sea, as he was known to scuttle boats, drown sailors and bind girls to rocks below the high water mark, but his name might remind us of the suggestion that Iona was Ì-shona, the blessed isle – or even Ì-Sheonaidh, the Island of Shony.

The nine maidens of old tutored heroes, as the Nine Witches of Gloucester trained Peredur in arms, or the great warrior-witch of Skye, Scàthach, trained the Irish heroes Cuchullain and Finn MacCool. We can well assume that the cauldron of initiation 'warmed' by such a sisterhood 'would not boil the food of a coward'.

Taliesin also tells us that as a young boy he was set to tend the cauldron of Ceridwen, who wished to bestow infinite wisdom on her ugly son. After keeping watch over the cauldron for a year,

Taliesin accidentally splashed himself with three drops of the liquor. In doing so, he had taken all the magical goodness of the cauldron – the remaining dregs were useless. In this story, the cauldron's contents are reminiscent of the All-Knowing Salmon – Eo Feasa – on which the Irish hero Finn MacCool burned his fingers while cooking the fish. As he put his thumb to his mouth, inspiration and universal knowledge dawned.

Is there any evidence at all of a cauldron of inspiration on Iona?

We know of a 'Pot of Iona' - Poit na h-Ì – by the loch a mile outside Fionnphort on the approach to the island. Is there anything on the island itself?

At the northern-most point of Iona, beyond **Cnoc an t-Suidhe** ('Hill of the Sitting', or perhaps 'Hill of the Couple') and a stone's throw from Sgeir nam Mart – is a rocky outcrop known as Dabhach – 'The Vat'. At the opposite end of the island, beyond Loch Staoneig, lies **Coire Sianta**, normally translated as 'charmed, or sacred, hollow' – yet 'coire' refers to a cauldron (or any geographical feature resembling a cauldron) and is cognate with the Welsh pair, meaning 'bath'. There is also, on the eastern side of the island, at **Tràigh Mór** – the 'Big Strand' – a cove once known as am Bruthas, meaning the 'broth' or brose, an oatmeal dish akin to porridge.

In the centre of the isle, beside Cnoc Mór, the Big Hill that stands above Iona Primary School and the Heritage Centre, we find **Bol Leithne**. If we assume 'Bol' to be a corruption of 'buaile', then this would refer to a circular enclosure for black cattle. If we take 'Bol' to stand for 'ból', then Bol Leithne would mean 'Eithne's Bowl'. The name is usually taken to refer to the mother of Columba, and yet there were other Eithnes, including an Irish Druidess of that name, and the first wife of Conn, King of Ireland.

Conn of the Hundred Battles was so fortunate in his first wife that the land enjoyed three harvests of corn every year. When Queen Eithne died, Conn married a fairy wife, and for a year the land knew neither corn nor milk. Conn's Druids sought for a sacrifice – "the son of a sinless couple" – but when all was readied a mysterious woman, or 'weird wife', appeared leading a cow and offering the beast in the boy's place. This would seem to be a myth – like that of Abraham and Isaac in the Bible – that explains the transition from human to animal sacrifice. One wonders whether the 'weird wife' wasn't Eithne herself, dead and therefore in faery form, and to find her associated with sacrificial cows raises questions about 'Eithne's Fold, or Enclosure'.

Thus far, we have enough to indicate that the goddess Bride, or Brigid, was worshipped on Iona, and the fact that the Christian church had to turn St. Bride into so prominent a figure as Christ's foster-mother suggests that a powerful cult existed before her canonization. Bride was associated with fire, fertility, craftwork and poetic inspiration, and was quite possibly worshipped by a select group of sacred virgins. She was associated with a sacred bowl or cauldron of initiation/inspiration, as well as with cattle and possibly sacrifice. In affecting to rid Iona of both women and cows, Columba was most probably taking action against 'witchcraft', for nowhere are witches deemed to be most problematic in the Hebrides than in their dealings with cattle.

Burial Sites

Iona's popularity as a place of burial would seem to go back a long way indeed, as suggested by Port nam Marbh on the south-eastern rump of Mull and the line of standing stones leading to Uamh nam Marbh facing Iona.

A short distance to the south and west of Martyr's Bay is **Cladh nan Druineach**, often translated as the 'Druid's Burial Ground', but more accurately the 'Burial Ground of the Craftsman, or Embroiderer'. More or less beside the burial ground, immediately in front of Martyr's Bay, is **an Ealadh** – the Mound, or the Tomb. It was here that the dead, being carried to Iona for burial, were rested, and Lucy Menzies in her 'Saint Columba of Iona' (1920) asserts that the bier was carried three times around an Ealadh in a sunwise direction before proceeding along the Street of the Dead. Ealadh can also signify learning or skill.

Cladh na Meirghe is situated beside **Cnoc na Meirghe**, meaning 'Hill of the Banner, or Signal'. This was believed to be a burial ground for unbaptized infants.

Cill Chainnich – the graveyard (chapel) of Kenneth – was close to the site of the Parish Church. An ancient cairn stands nearby.

Alongside **Clachanach** ('Field of Stones'), beyond the abbey, is the site of Cill mo Neachdain. Of this burial site there was an age-old saying:

Thiodhlaic mi mo naoi nighnean mar sheachdnar an Cill mo Neachdain ann an I.

"I buried my nine daughters in seven in the graveyard of my Nechtan in Iona." The statement would suggest nine daughters interred in seven burials.

There were several kings of the Picts named Nechtan. One, the legends tell us, had been forced from his kingdom and, whilst in exile, asked Brigid to pray for him. She prophesied that he would return in peace to his kingdom. When this happened, Nechtan dedicated a church to her in Fifeshire, and her fame spread across Scotland.

At Dún Nechtain – 'Nechtan's Fort' – in Angus, King Ecgfrith of Northumberland was defeated and killed on 20th May 685. He was buried on Iona.

There is another Nechtan in Irish myth. This is the god of wisdom and water, husband of Boand, the 'Bride of the Waters', whose name means 'Cow-Wealth'. On the hill of Nechtan (Sìdh-Nechtan) there was a holy well where dwelt the Salmon of Wisdom. Only Nechtan and three cup-bearers had access to this well.

Of the nine daughters buried in seven, we may sense a genuine family tragedy – and yet the numbers alone should give us pause for thought.

Nine would seem to be a typical number of priestesses of the goddess, a number arrived at by multiplying the triple form of the goddess (maiden, mother, crone) by itself. From the island known as Sena, we are led to believe that an annual sacrifice disposed of one of the nine. The Irish voyager Ruadh ('Red') discovered an underwater island, north of Ireland, inhabited by nine beautiful women who slept on nine bronze beds and whose eyes shone with rainbow light. He spent nine nights with them, and they communally bore him a son, but when he forgot to visit them at the end of his voyage they chased him, kicking his son's severed head before them 'like a football'.

Seven is a number of special significance: in the Book of Genesis we read of Joseph – who, with his coat of many colours, represents an authentically shamanic, if not Druidic, character – interpreting Pharaoh's dream of seven years of great plenty followed by seven years of famine. (Joseph, we remember, was cast into a pit by his brothers and left for dead, recollecting a form of initiation). Celtic kingship seems to have been an office that expired after seven years, at which point the king's magical vitality would appear to have waned. King Arthur, when he had become the Maimed King, caused seven years of sterility wherever he set his foot. In Ireland, three Kings of Ulster agreed to rule in rotation, and as 'pledges' or hostages they gave seven chieftains who would be burned as sacrifices if one of the kings did not step down at the end of seven years. We might wonder whether the Arch-Druid's prophecy over Brìde – "when for the seventh time the sacred year has come" – refers to seven cycles of seven years.

To what, then, might the burial of nine daughters in seven allude? Much would depend upon who uttered the grim remark, but if we take Nechtan to refer to the exiled Pictish king associated with Brìde (rather than, say, the Nechtan of the southern Picts who banished the monks from Iona in 716) then perhaps we have a burial ground that was dedicated to Brìde, and nine daughters 'of the goddess' interred there during one cycle of kingship. The legends insist that Brìde grew up on the south-eastern slopes of Dùn Ì, in the vicinity of Cill mo Neachdain, and in the shadow of the natural 'cauldron' formed by Dùn Ì itself and its Tobar na h-Aoise, meaning 'Well of Age, or Antiquity', or perhaps 'Well of the People' (aois-dàna – 'people of special skill: poets'). This is eerily similar to the Hill of Nechtan and its well of knowledge. Nechtan's chapel suggests the conflation of a Pictish king blessed by Bride and the Irish water-god married to Boand, 'She of the White Cows'.

Dùn Mhanannain

On the west coast of Iona, standing over the beautiful Port Bàn ('White Port', or 'Fair Port') is **Dùn-Bhuirg**, which means 'Hill of the Fort' (or, more literally, 'Fort-Fort'). Glass beads and pottery discovered at the site of this hill fort can be dated from the first century BCE to the third century CE, although it may well have been occupied earlier. The presence of the Iron Age fortress, with a defensive stone wall on the landward side and small circular stone huts, would suggest a single tribal community living on the island at least six hundred years before Columba landed.

To the north is Nead a' Ghille Ruaidh – 'Nest of the Reddish Lad' – perhaps Ruadh of the nine beautiful women, and Port an Duine Mhairbh – 'Port of the Dead Man' – beyond which we find **Dùn Mhanannain**, 'Fort of Manannan'.

Manannan was a god of the sea – the son of the Irish sea-god Lir (Welsh: Llyr). He was a warrior, noble and handsome, who rode the waves in an enchanted horse-drawn boat called "Wave Sweeper". He was renowned as a magician and craftsman, his shamanic cloak of many colours causing forgetfulness. Irish myth tells us of an Eithne who acted as maid to Manannan's daughter. After a chieftain of the Tuatha de Danaan tried to rape her, Eithne refused to eat or drink. Manannan, and the Irish love god Aonghus (the illegitimate son of Boand), searched for a remedy as far as India, where Manannan found two magic cows whose milk never ran dry. Thus was Eithne sustained. This again indicates a pagan cult connecting women and cattle, and perhaps accounts for Bol Leithne, the bowl or enclosure of Eithne's sacred cows.

Manannan ruled in Tìr Tairngire, the 'Land of Promise', an island somewhere in the Atlantic Ocean which – like Arthur's Avalon – was associated with apples. Here his daughter Niamh of the Golden Hair lived happily with the poet Oisin, bearing him a daughter named Plùr nam Ban, 'Flower of the Woman'. In his Welsh form, Manawydan was the brother of Branwen and Bran the Blessed.

Bran, whose name means 'Raven', allowed his sister Branwen to marry the Irish king Matholwch. When hostilities broke out, Bran restored the peace by presenting Ireland with a magic cauldron that could bring the dead back to life, although it would deprive them of speech. This compares with the cauldron of initiation, the 'bowl' or 'bath' (Welsh: pair) that would not allow the initiate to speak of their new-found knowledge. Branwen was ill-treated in Ireland and forced to work as a cook, during which time she reared a starling, which in Gaelic is 'druid', and trained the bird to recognise her brother. The message sent alerted Bran the Blessed to his sister's plight, and the invasion of Ireland began.

The Irish possession of the cauldron spelled disaster for the British. Only seven returned. Bran was mortally wounded, but instructed his companions to cut off his head, which continued to eat, drink and entertain his comrades during their prolonged journey home. Later versions of the story assert that Bran's head was buried at Tower Hill in London to protect Britain from invasion.

Another Bran is the hero of a marvellous Irish voyage. Discovering a silver branch covered with white flowers, Bran mac Febal was visited by a fairy woman who told him of the wonderful islands beyond the sea, inhabited by beautiful women who knew neither sorrow, nor sickness, nor death. As Bran and his companions set sail they encountered Manannan, who again told them of the marvels that lay ahead.

After finding the Island of Merriment, they reached the Isle of Women, whose lovely leader tricked them ashore with an enchanted thread. Here the heroes lived in luxury for what they thought was a year, until they felt it was time to return. The leader of the women warned them not to set foot on land. On arriving home in Ireland, they first discovered that they had been away for many years and were already considered heroes of legend. When one of them leapt ashore he immediately disintegrated into ashes.

Another place-name mentioned in Ritchie's 1928 survey of Iona is the now obsolete Cill mo Ghobhannan, which means 'Cell of my Govannon'. Govannon (Irish: Goibhniu) was the god of smiths and metalworkers, a trade strongly associated with magic by the Celts (St Patrick is said to have prayed for protection "against spells of women and smiths and druids"). In his Irish form he was one of the Tuatha de Danaan – the People of Danu. He could create a perfect sword or spear with just three blows of his magic hammer. Brigid's son Ruadan stabbed the smith god with a spear before a battle. Govannon, or Goibhniu, merely plucked the spear from his side and mortally wounded the son of Brigid. Cill mo Ghobhannan suggests a shrine to the god of smiths, just as Cill mo Neachdain might indicate a shrine to the water-god with his well of knowledge.

Taliesin referred to a "Cauldron of the ruler of the deep" – Nechtan, perhaps, if not the mighty Manannan himself – that was gently warmed by the breath of nine maidens. We know also that the sisterhood of Bride (who patronized poets and craftsmen) tended a sacred fire and that priestesses trained heroes and perhaps put them through an initiation that involved a magical cauldron. This could have been a 'bath' of initiation or a magical brew that imparted 'wisdom'. Bride, as Brigid, is often conflated with Anu, or Danu, the mother-goddess of the Tuatha de Danaan. As a Christian saint, she was known as 'Christ's Milkmaid', and the cows of her convent at Kildare never ran dry of milk. Latha fhèill Bride is the festival of Candlemas – Imbolc – when according to a traditional rhyme, 'The Queen shall come from the mound'. As the goddess who inspired poetry, she was the guardian of the Cauldron.

The Fairy Mounds

Heading westwards, the island's road terminates at A' Mhachair beside **Camus Cùl an Taibh**, which usually translates as the 'Bay at the Back of the Ocean'. Taibh in Gaelic signifies 'substance'. Aibheis is the sea – the 'abyss' – and both aibhse and taibhse refer to goblins, spirits or visions. Cnoc Urrais looks down on the bay from the north-east: it translates as 'Hill of the Brownie' (urraisg: 'monster' or 'idiot'), which might also relate to the ùruisg, a water-spirit, for the area around Cnoc Urrais includes **Na Glughtraichean**, which means something like 'Places of the Rumbling Ebb'.

Where the road ends, just to the right is **Sìthean Beag**, the Little Fairy Mound. On the left-hand side is the rise sometimes known as Cnoc nam Aingeal, but locally it is called the Big Fairy Mound: **Sìthean Mór**.

Adomnàn writes of "a certain Brother, a cunning and prying man" who resolved to spy on Columba when the saint desired to go alone to the western plain known as The Machair. This disobedient monk positioned himself on a hillock – possibly that known as Cnoc Odhráin – Oran's Hill – and watched as Columba mounted Sìthean Mór and prayed 'with hands spread out to heaven':

"... For holy angels, the citizens of the heavenly kingdom, were flying down with amazing speed, dressed in white robes, and began to gather around the holy man as he prayed. After they had conversed a little with St Columba, the heavenly crowd – as though they could feel that they were being spied on – quickly returned to the heights of heaven."

In this way the monks converted the Big Fairy Mound into the Angels' Knoll.

There is a tradition that the isle once contained numerous standing stones and that a 'small green hill' formed a 'Druidic temple of twelve stones, each with a human body buried beneath it'. Richard Pococke, bishop of Lismore, visited the island in 1760, and told the traveller Thomas Pennant that on the Eve of St. Michael's Day (29th September) the islanders brought their horses to this small hill on which stood a cairn surrounded by a circle of stones, and led the horses thrice round the hill in a sunwise direction.

In the twentieth century, the mound was the death of one young Italian woman. Marie Emily Fornario apparently fell in love with the island. She took to visiting the lonelier places, researching the folklore and writing mystical poetry. One day, she announced that she had to leave the island immediately. Her bags were packed and carried to the jetty, but it being a Sunday no ferry was plying the Sound. She returned to her lodgings and decided that it was no longer necessary for her to leave Iona.

A day or two later, her naked body was found beside the Big Fairy Mound. She was clutching a knife, with which she had apparently tried to open the Sìthean. She was buried in Reilig Odhráin. A poem by Helen B. Cruikshank, entitled "Lost Ladye?", describes her moonlit walk:

> The sheen o' steel was in her hand,
> The sheen o' stars in her een,
> An' she wad open the fairy hill
> An' she wad let oot the queen.

Fiona Macleod relates the story told to him by an old woman of Iona named Giorsal whose daughter, Ealàsaidh, had gone missing. She had last been seen "laughing an' talking to the reeds" in the swamp by Staoneig in the south of the island. Her mother insisted that "For months a monk had come to her o' nights in her sleep, an' said he would kill her, because she was a heathen," the old monks hating "folk from the North, an' women-folk above all."

Receiving no succour from the church, the girl visited old Mary Gillespie – "her that has the sight an' a power o' the old wisdom" – who lived by Lochan Poit na h-Ì beyond Fionnphort. "After that," said Giorsal, "she took to meeting friends in the moonshine" ... "Up between Sgéur Iolaire and Cnoc Druidean there's a path that no monk can go. There, in the old days, they burned a woman. She was not a woman ... She was one o' the Sorrows of the Sheen ... It's ill that brings harm to them. That's why the monks are na strong over by Staoneig way."

The south end of the island, so Peter Underwood recounts in his 'Gazetteer of Scottish Ghosts', "has an evil reputation locally". He refers to a resident who mentioned "crowds of elementals" – supernatural entities or forces – populating the south, and a smell of death that hangs there. Adomnán wrote "Of a fierce fight with demons in which St Columba received timely help from the angels" when Columba had set off 'into the wilder parts of the island'. Could this also have been in the south?

Sròn Iolaire – 'Eagle's Nose' – lies a short distance to the south of Sìthean Mór, and the Hill of the Starlings – Cnoc nan Druidean – a little way beyond; the path 'that no monk can go' possibly the 'Pass of the Woman'. What are we to make of all these tales of disappearing girls, battles between angels and demons, crowds of elementals and the Faery burned by the monks?

A sacrifice by burning may well recall an ancient rite. The hostages of the three Kings of Emania in Ulster were threatened with burning if a king ruled beyond his allotted seven years. Brìde's association with a sacred fire may betray a hint of darker rituals. Certainly, it would seem that folk memory recollects grim practices to the south of Sìthean Mór and some kind of belief that the south end was haunted and unholy.

It is recorded that when Columba and his companions landed on Iona, the saint was met by two 'Druids' disguised as bishops. Columba saw through them instantly, denounced them and 'burned their books'. That there was an impressive library on Iona we know from the historian Boece's statement that Fergus II of Scotland struck a treaty with Alaric the Goth in 410; together they plundered Rome and Fergus brought back a chest of books to add to the collection that already existed on the isle (Fergus, it seems, previously went to Iona for his coronation). This happened over 150 years before Columba's arrival. Exactly who were the librarians of Iona in the fifth century is unclear, although we know that the Irish Druids of Nechtan were keepers of the ancient oghams (Celtic scripts) and libraries. That Columba – a lover of books – should burn the books of the Druids suggests that Druidic practices were the norm when the saint arrived.

On the east coast of the island, far to the south above the Marble Quarry, we find **Sìthean Mór na h'Àird**, the 'Big Fairy Mound of the Height'. Like the other mounds, this was deemed to be the abode of fairies and was thus associated with a cult of the ancestors who inhabited these mounds in a condition between living and dead.

Two Lowland folktales preserve elements of faery lore. There is, intriguingly, a Tobhta nan Sassunaich, or the '(Ruined) House of the Lowlanders' close by the Sìthean Mór na h'Àird, and Grass Point on the eastern side of Mull where the 'pilgrim route' to Iona commences is also given as Port an t-Sasunnaich: the Lowlanders' Port. Were these rites brought to Iona by the Britons of Strathclyde or the Brigantes – the People of Brigantia – from the Border region?

Tam Lin is a traditional tale set in the Scottish borders. Lady Janet, the Laird of Carterhaugh's daughter, encounters Tam Lin at a well in a fairy wood. She summons him by picking a white rose. In Giorsal's tale of her missing daughter, as told to Fiona Macleod, the girl Ealàsaidh came home one night "smiling an' pluckin' wild roses":

'"Breisleach!" I cried, "what's the meanin' o' roses in January?" She looked at me, frighted, an' said nothin', but threw the things on the fire. It was next day she went away.' (Breisleach: 'raving', 'delirium')

Tam Lin shows Janet all the flowers of the forest and then lets her head home. Intrigued by this man, Janet in time returns to the well and, summoning Tam Lin, demands to know whether he is a Christian or one of the fairy folk.

Tam Lin tells her his tale: at the age of nine he was taken to the home of his grandfather, the Earl of Roxburgh. On the way, he was lulled into a deep sleep by the cold north wind and fell from his horse onto a green knoll. The Queen of Fairies spirited him away and has kept him in thrall for seven years. Tam Lin is deeply worried, for every seven years the Fairy Queen 'pays a human tithe to hell' and he's fearful that he will be the next sacrifice. However, Hallowe'en – the old Celtic festival of Samhain – is upon them, a time when the gates to the Otherworld are opened. Tam Lin gives Janet instructions as to how she might rescue him.

At the midnight hour, Janet watches as the Queen leads her elfin troop through the wood. Tam Lin rides the third horse, which is milk-white. On cue, Janet grabs hold of him and holds on tight as the fairies screech and the man in her arms goes through a series of transformations, to a newt or eel, a serpent, a bear, a lion and a bolt of red-hot iron. Finally, he changes into a 'mother-naked man', at which point she casts her green mantle over him (à la 'Brigid of the Green Mantle'), plunging him into either a trough of milk or the well itself, from which Tam Lin emerges free of his enchantment.

The magical transformations and the final baptism in a bath of milk or a well are suggestive of the kind of initiation that the Welsh bard Taliesin underwent. We know that the priestesses of Sena were deemed capable of shape-shifting, as was the protean sea-god Manannan. Fiona Macleod recounts a tale that Manannan so loved a beautiful woman of the south, whose name was Sunshine, that he brought her to Iona one September, but in the winter months she began to pine. Manannan turned her into a seal by night and, by day, a woman sleeping in his dùn. Manannan was the forerunner of that most Celtic of saints, the archangel Michael, whose feast day is in September.

In the traditional tale of Thomas Rhymer, the Laird of Ercildoune is a gifted harpist, charmer and weaver of songs: in other words, a bard. As he played his harp one day by the Eildon Tree, he saw a lady clad all in green, riding a milk-white steed. Greeting her, he discovers that she is the 'Queen of fair Elfland', who desires to kiss him. One kiss of her lips, she tells him, will condemn him to her service for seven years, during which time he must not utter a single word.

At the end of his seven years, the Queen offers Thomas his freedom. Her parting gift is an apple from her orchard that confers on Thomas the gifts of truth and prophecy. So Thomas returns to Ercildoune to become a famous seer, although his mind is forever returning to the Queen of Elfland, until one night he hears of a white doe grazing nearby. Knowing that this is a harbinger of the Otherworld, Thomas sets out to find the faery deer and is never seen again.

Both tales repeat the 'seven year rule' that we have examined already, suggesting that the king's seven year reign was part of his contract with the goddess: the 'Fairy Queen'. Thomas Rhymer's time in Elfland is also, quite clearly, an initiatory experience. The injunction against speaking reminds us of the Cauldron of Rebirth that will restore warriors to life but deprive them of the power of speech.

The king – or the initiate – is obliged to spend seven years in service to the 'Queen', the goddess of the land who is also the Queen of the Dead: Brigid (Brìde) in her light and dark aspects.

The sacred marriage of the king to the land was seen as a mating with the goddess and a contract with the Otherworldly realm of Faerie. The small green hills or burial mounds are vestiges of this faith in the inter-relatedness of the human and fairy worlds, the living and the dead. Kingly power and poetic inspiration were both the gifts of Faerie, and the Fairy Queen is none other than the goddess herself, the Lady of the Shores, Brighid bhòidheach, Brìde the beautiful, who "shall come from the mound" on her feast day in ceud mhìos an earraich, the first month of Spring.

The Black Stones

The Black Stones of Iona appear to have been situated roughly where the Iona Community's shop now stands, under **Cnoc nan Carnan**, or 'Hill of the Stones'. Ritchie records the tradition that there was only one stone, "which was destroyed early in the 18th Century by a fanatic who believed that it bewitched the people."

They were not black – but black was the doom believed to fall on anyone who broke an oath sworn on them.

The Stone of Destiny was believed to be one of these stones, and upon it Columba reputedly crowned Áedán mac Gabráin king of Dál Riata. According to legend, the Stone was later removed to Dunstaffnage, and thence to Scone, where the kings of Scotland were then crowned, until Edward I took it south to Westminster Abbey in 1296. For centuries, the Stone rested beneath the coronation chair, and every English monarch was crowned upon it, until it was finally returned to Scotland at the end of the twentieth century. It is said that moving the Stone of Destiny signals the end of the ruling dynasty. One version of the legend asserts that the Stone was originally the stone pillow on which Jacob slept at Bethel, receiving his vision of a ladder that reached towards heaven.

That it was allegedly brought over by tribes migrating from the Middle East helps to preserve its exotic, mystical aura as well as acknowledging the migrations of the Celtic peoples and the similarities between Druidic doctrines and those of Egypt and the Mediterranean. Besides, it is no more bizarre than the story told to Fiona Macleod by a man of Tiree that Mary Magdalene lies buried in a cave on Iona. It also relates the Stone to those other 'black stones' worshipped in the Middle East, and in particular to the Ka'aba, Islam's holiest of holies. This 'black' stone once enshrined Al-Uzza, an aspect of the Great Goddess of Arabia – a moon goddess. The Ka'aba is served by men – instead of priestesses – known as Beni Shaybah: 'Sons of the Old Woman'.

The Stone of Destiny is clearly related to the Lia Fàil of Ireland. Brought from the Isle of Fal ('Destiny') or 'city of Falias' by the Tuatha de Danaan, the Lia Fàil stood near the "Mound of Hostages" at Tara. There it cried out whenever the true king stood on it, thereby constituting the ultimate test for would-be kings of Ireland.

In the Bodleian Library can be found a verse in crude Latin which reads:

In Eqypt, Moses preached to the people, saying
That Scota, the fairy maiden, who is the stone,
Told of the strange manner in which the land
should be conquered.

Princess Scota was "the daughter of Pharoah" who brought the stone to Ireland. In another version of the story it is the son of the King of Spain who brought the royal seat to Tara, whence it was carried to Scotland and brought to Iona by Fergus Mór. Both stories reveal an insight into the migrations of the Iberian Celts, tracing their lineage back to North Africa. In a similar vein is the myth of Cesair, Noah's granddaughter, who sailed for seven years with her father Bith before they reached Ireland. Cesair married Fintan, the only one of them to survive the Flood because he managed to turn himself into a salmon, thereby also giving his name to the Salmon of Wisdom that basks in Nechtan's Well. The oddly-named **Sgeir Chaesar** – 'Caesar's Rock' – at the extreme north-east of the island might more appropriately be called 'Cesair's Skerry'.

The rhyme above also allies the Stone of Destiny with Faery and suggests that it housed an oracular spirit, here given as 'Scota', the mythical goddess of Scotland.

Are we to believe that the stone itself screamed when the true king set foot on it – or might not a priestess, entranced or 'possessed' by the stone's spirit, the goddess, have shrieked at the given moment? The Celts drew prophesies from the screams of ravens and eagles, and the cries of the banshee, or 'fairy woman', were associated with each royal line in Ireland: even the royal house of Stuart appears to have had its own banshee or guardian spirit. Furthermore, the banshee is associated with Badb, a goddess of battle whose name means 'crow'. Bran, he whose prophetic head nestled in its magical dish, means 'raven'. The hill which overlooks the site of the Black Stones on Iona is called Sgùrr an Fhithich – the Raven's Peak – so that the scream of the Stone of Destiny was the cry of the raven, the goddess of battle, the Great Queen ('Mórrigan'), the fairy woman who attached herself to the ruling dynasty. Brìde, or Brigid, also seems to have been a patroness of warfare ('Briga') whose warriors were known as 'brigands'.

We know that one method for divining the new king was the Tarbfeis, the dream that came after the sacrifice of a bull and the meal or bath made from its flesh; it is likely that the dreamer was also wrapped in the bull's hide. The next step was the ritual marriage of the king to the goddess. In one version, the new king was offered a chalice containing water drawn from a sacred well by a beautiful girl who personified the goddess and was most likely sacrificed. There are a number of wells and springs on Iona, including the Well of Antiquity (or 'the People') on Dùn Ì and the stream known as Sruth a' Mhuilinn that runs past Burnside Cottage close to the Hill of the Stones. The new king might have copulated with the representative of the goddess before her sacrifice. Gerald of Wales records a thirteenth century ritual in Ulster in which the new king mated with a white mare, after which the horse was killed, its flesh put into a cooking pot in which the king bathed, and then the meat shared out among the assembly. In this instance, the horse is the goddess in equine ('milk-white') form.

We might wonder whether the Stone of Destiny was also the sacrificial block on which the girl representing the goddess was sacrificed. We are close to Cill mo Neachdain here – Nechtan with his hill-top well to which only he and his three cup-bearers had access – and we are in the territory of Bride, growing up on the south-east slope of Dùn Ì. We are also within spitting distance of **Cnoc nam Marbh**, or 'Hill of the Dead', at a site fit for the coronation and burial of kings.

A truly odd Gaelic rhyme of old was published by Alexander Nicholson in 1881. It goes by the title 'Tuireadh Brighid' – "Lament for Brighid":

"I call and pray to you, stone,
Release not Brighid.
For she sours the drink,
To many a good man (or warrior) without fault
Has she brought death.
Since your thirst now exceeds thirstiness,
May there be an eternal thirst upon you, Brighid."
(trans. Duncan MacLeod)

This sounds like a curse upon the Brigid of warfare, the dark and wintry cailleach, the pagan moon goddess associated with ravens and the 'stone'.

Martin Martin, writing in about 1695, identified the Black Stones as lying to the west of 'Dùn nam Manach' – the 'Monks' Fort', now known as Tòrr Abb – and stated that Macdonald, 'King of the Isles', "delivered the rights of their lands to his vassals in the isles and continent, with uplifted hands and bended knees, on the black stones".

Oran

Before we leave the Island of Druids, we should examine the crossover from pagan to Christian activity on Iona. The charge was to some extent led by Brìde as she was converted from the Goddess of the New Moon to the Mother of the King of Glory. And yet it is in the curious legend of Òran ('song' or 'glee' in modern Gaelic) that the Druidical and the Christian worlds clash most oddly.

Adomnán does not mention him, although he does refer to "a soldier of Christ called Máel Odrain", or 'follower of Odran'. 'The Book of Ballymote' (circa 1391) lists "Odhran of Iona, of severe piety" and the seventeenth-century 'Annals of the Four Masters' contain his obituary for 548 – fifteen years before Columba arrived. The eighth-century 'Martyrology of Oenghus the Culdee' gives his feast-day as the 27th October, close to Samhain, the Celtic Hallowe'en. The island of Oronsay is named after him, as are Iona's oldest surviving building, the royal burial ground, a well and the hill from which the prying monk is said to have observed Columba conversing with angels.

In the earliest version of the Oran legend (Irish, twelfth century) Columba announces to his company: "It would benefit us if our roots were put down into the ground here ... Someone among you should go down into the soil of the island to consecrate it." A later version, recorded at the end of the seventeenth century, describes Columba dreaming that a famine "would never cease unless he buried a man alive." Other traditions assert that Columba was unable to found his church because an evil spirit tore down the walls as fast as they were built.

Whether he volunteered or was chosen by lot – as sacrificial victims often were – it was Oran to whom Columba said, "I shall give you the kingdom of God ... and I shall give you this, that no one who makes a request at my tomb or my resting-place will be granted it unless he first seek it of you." In other words, the entrance to Columba's sacred precinct was to be guarded by St Oran.

Oran was buried alive. In the version of 1698, he was buried upright and his grave opened again after twenty-four hours. The 1771 retelling, drawing on local tradition, states:

"Three days afterwards Columba opened the grave to see what might be the fate of his friend. Oran opened his swimming eyes and said

> Cha'n bhuill am bàs na iongantas
> Na iofroin mar a teistonas

'There is no wonder in death, nor is hell as it is reported.'"

Columba called out in a great hurry:

> Ùir, ùir air sùil Òrain
> Mar labhair è tuille còmhradh

'Earth, earth on the eye of Oran, lest he speak any more'

The notion of a burial or sacrifice consecrating a sacred building (to 'sacrifice' means 'to make sacred') is nothing unusual. Under each of the twelve stones that once stood on Sìthean Mór a body was said to be buried (we recall Brighid, who has brought death to many a good man without fault). Numerous legends surround religious sites and the problems of building there, reflecting the fact that Pope Gregory charged his missionaries with erecting their churches on pagan shrines. We can readily accept that the first church of Columba was built on a site of pagan worship – but how can we account for the Christian saint himself initiating the sacrifice of a saint who had apparently died fifteen years earlier?

The story is reminiscent of an initiation. That Oran is 'dead' for three days reminds us of Lazarus, and Christ himself, and Jonah in the belly of the whale. The three days derive from the dark of the moon, a period associated with death and rebirth and connected to the menses in women.

We know that the cauldron of rebirth sent by Bran ('Raven') to Ireland deprived the initiate of the power of speech. That Oran came out blabbing sealed his fate, for the initiated should not speak of their experiences. Was Oran in fact an initiate into a cult? Does the legend dimly remember initiatory ceremonies on Iona? Was some such ceremony conducted by Columba, or does the story indicate his ending of the practice? When Columba dispelled an 'evil spirit' from a pail of milk, was he in fact purifying a bath or trough of milk used in pagan initiation and healing ceremonies?

Magical cauldrons abound in Celtic mythology: Irish accounts of the battle of Mag Roth, which took place in 637, refer to them. Their existence is felt in the chalice offered by the girl to the new king, in the pot that boiled the flesh of the bull or the horse, in the fairy well or bath of milk into which Janet dipped Tam Lin, in the cauldron of inspiration and the cauldron of rebirth. In their final manifestation, they appear as the Grail, which is variously a dish, a goblet, or – according to Wolfram von Eschenbach – a stone. The poet Kenneth Macleod, writing early in the twentieth century, referred to Iona as 'my Grail-lit Isle' and:

> "Iona the blest, I mo chridh thu,
> Isle of my heart, my grail."

The time of St Columba was also the time of Arthur, Merlin and Taliesin. It was a period of confusion following the end of the Roman occupation of Britain: the British tribes were fending off attacks by the Saxons and the Picts, and the Irish Scots were consolidating their hold on Dál Riata (roughly, modern-day

Argyll) in the land of the Picts, who were named by the Romans Pictii, or 'Painted Ones'. As well as the battles for land there were battles for faith. Iona lay on the fault-line between Dál Riata and Pictland, and there is some indication that the Picts had reclaimed the island before Columba arrived. Was Oran the last to undergo a Druidic initiation?

The Preiddeu Annwn or 'Spoils of Annwn' describes Arthur's epic journey to the Otherworld in search of the Treasures of Britain, and especially the cauldron of the chief of Annwn, which was warmed by the breath of nine maidens. Taliesin ends the poem:

> "Monks pack together howling like wolves
> From an encounter with masters who know.
> They do not know when twilight and dawn divide,
> Nor what the course of the wind, who agitates it,
> What place it ravages, on what region it roars.
> The grave of the saint is vanishing from the foot of the altar."

The whole poem reads as an initiatory experience which, like Bran's adventure in Ireland, leaves only seven survivors. Elsewhere, Taliesin declares that, "Perfect is my seat in Caer Sidi" – a faery fort or temple:

> "Plague and age hurt him not who's in it ...
> About its points are ocean's streams:
> And the abundant well above it –
> Sweeter than white wine the drink in it."

He could almost be describing Iona: the 'Hill of the Sitting' at the north end, hard by the Rock of the Cow-to-be-Slaughtered, and the Skerry of Cesair, Noah's granddaughter – associated with the dove and the All-Knowing Salmon that swims in the fountain of Manannan's otherworldly palace, in the Well of the People of Anu, poets extraordinaire – and where Bride's fire is tended by maidens in the sacred enclosure.

Brigantia, Brigid or Brìde may be the origin for that beautiful girl from the south – Deàrrsadh-na-Ghréine: 'Sunshine' – whom

Manannan took to his dùn on the island in September, at the time of his festival which later became Michaelmas. Brìde's festival was Imbolc – she was the sun in its strength as he was the sea and winter, to whom the islanders sacrificed a bowl of porridge every Maundy Thursday. But the bowl was also Brìde's cauldron, and she is akin to Manannan's daughter, Niamh of the Golden Hair, who loved Oisin the poet in the Land of Promise.

Nechtan's well, high up on Dùn Ì, was both a magical cauldron and the home of the mythical Salmon, Eo Feasa. The Salmon was eaten by the warrior Finn MacCool, whose son was Oisin. Nechtan was married to Boand, the Bride of the Waters, goddess of cattle. As Brìde to Manannan, so Boand to Nechtan. Goibhniu, the god of craftsmen and armourers, mortally wounded Ruadan, causing the first keening to be heard in Ireland and transforming Brigid into the banshee, the original Pietà, for she was also the mother-goddess, patroness of the gifted, and she nurtured the Light of the World in the bleak midwinter.

The salmon, the cauldron, the cup of the waters, the bloody spear, the Stone of Destiny and the mystical dove all lead in time to the Grail, for they are associated with divine kingship, poetic inspiration and the contract with the faery realm of the dead, as was the Isle of the Yew Trees herself: Ì nam ban bòidheach.

Manannan's Land of Promise was also – like the mythical Avallon – associated with apples. The Druid Myrddin (the original Merlin), who went mad at the Battle of Arderydd in 573 and fled into the Caledonian forest, sang a poem – 'Afallenau', or 'Apple-trees' – in praise of a "Sweet apple tree ...

> "When I was in my right mind I used to have at its foot
> A fair wanton maiden, one slender and queenly."

He also laments his nineteen apple trees. The following poem was written by William Butler Yeats in 1897 and draws heavily on Celtic beliefs:

> I went out to the hazel wood,
> Because a fire was in my head,
> And cut and peeled a hazel wand,

And hooked a berry to a thread;
And when white moths were on the wing,
And moth-like stars were flickering out,
I dropped the berry in a stream
And caught a little silver trout.

When I had laid it on the floor
I went to blow the fire aflame,
But something rustled on the floor,
And some one called me by my name;
It had become a glimmering girl
With apple blossom in her hair
Who called me by my name and ran
And faded through the brightening air.

Though I am old with wandering
Through hollow lands and hilly lands,
I will find out where she has gone,
And kiss her lips and take her hands;
And walk among long dappled grass,
And pluck till time and times are done
The silver apples of the moon,
The golden apples of the sun.

There is a shamanic initiation in this. Nine hazels of poetry grow over the sacred well in Manannan's palace; every seventh year, in mid June, the nuts drop into the well and travel up the river Boyne ("I buried my nine daughters in seven in the graveyard of my Nechtan on Iona"). There is both a 'Nut Hill' and Geodha Cnoc-a-chno ('Nut Hill Creek') along the coast from Dùn Mhanannain. The 'little silver trout' is clearly related to the Eo Feasa, the All-Knowing Salmon who swallowed the poetic hazelnuts. The faery girl who calls to the poet is surely Niamh, an aspect of Brìde or Brigid – 'Breò-Saighead': 'Fire-Arrow'. The moon travels in what is known as a nineteen-year Metonic cycle: 235 full moons equate to nineteen solar years. The sacred fire of Brighid at her shrine of Kildare was tended by nineteen priestesses who each ruled (i.e. personified the goddess) for a year. The 'silver apples of the moon', Merlin's nineteen apple trees, and the nineteen priestesses of Brighid might make us wonder whether the priestesses were familiarly known as 'apples' in recognition of their connection to the Moon – in which case the 'Island of Apples' (Avalon) might in fact be the island of the priestesses of the Moon, or Brìde. The modern Gaelic for 'apple' is ubhal, from the Early Irish ubull or uball. Could Iona therefore have been **Ì-Ubhalach**: the 'apple-bearing island', Manannan's 'Land of Promise'?

The earliest reference to 'Arthur' comes in Book I, Chapter 9 of Adomnán's 'Life of St Columba'. This refers to the sons of Áedán mac Gabráin, and the saint's prophecy that Artuir, along with two of his brothers, will not succeed their father: "They will all be slaughtered by enemies and fall in battle". Áedán was the first king to be crowned by Columba on Iona in 574, the year after Merlin went mad.

This Artuir – whose name could derive from 'Artu' or 'Artos', signifying 'bear', or the Old Irish 'art', meaning 'stone' – appears to have fought at the head of an alliance of Scottish and British kings against the Northumbrian Saxons and the Picts. At this time, the southern region of Scotland was British and Welsh-speaking. According to Adomnán, Artuir died in a battle against the Miathi, a Pictish tribe, somewhere in the region of Stirling. The eleventh-century "Annals of Tigernach" also record Artuir, son of Áedán, dying in battle and gives the year as 596.

The 'Martyrology of Oenghus' records Áedán as also having a daughter named Muirgein, or Morgan: 'born of the sea'. Certain genealogies give Artuir's mother as one Ygerna del Acqs, whose parents were Viviane and Taliesin. Furthermore, Artuir is said to have married one Gwenhwyfar, or Guinevere of Rheged. How far these genealogies wander into the realms of fantasy is hard to say – what we do have is a prince named Arthur fighting with the British in the sixth-century, whose sister was Morgan, and who died in battle near Stirling. He was not a king, but a warlord, as the earliest chronicles describe him. Centuries after his death he was to be transformed into the greatest hero of the British Isles: the Once and Future King, who set his holy knights on a quest for the Grail – this "Arthur of mournful memory", in Taliesin's words, who sought the wondrous cauldron in the time of Columba.

His father was crowned on Iona ... can we not imagine Arthur's remains carried to the Island of Beautiful Women, that burial place of kings?

Pictish Boar Carving

ISLAND of SAINTS
Door in St. Orans Chapel
1 Abbey
2 Bishop's Walk
3 Carn Cùl ri Eirinn
4 Cladh an Diseirt
5 Cnoc Cùil Phail
6 Gleann Teampuill
7 Iomaire nan Achd
8 Maclean's Cross
9 Nunnery
10 Port a' Churaich
11 Port nam Mairtear
12 Port Rónáin
13 Reilig Odhráin
14 St Oran's Chapel
15 Tòrr Abb
16 Tràigh Bàn nam Manach
17 Uamh nan Calman
1
2
3
4
5
6
7
8
9
10
11
12
13
14
15
16
17

IONA

Island of Saints

Island of Saints

Chalum-chille nam feart 's nan tuam
- "Columcille of the graves and tombs"
(Carmina Gadelica)

The ferry from Mull arrives at the modern jetty, constructed in 1977 between two sandy bays. To the right lies **Port Rónáin**, 'Ronan's Bay'. St Rónán was an Irish saint whose evangelical career began on Iona. His reach seems to have extended as far as North Rona, beyond the Butt of Lewis in the Outer Hebrides. The chapel adjoining the Nunnery on Iona is dedicated to him.

Rónán's most famous encounter was with the 'wildman' Suibhne Geilt. King Suibhne (pronounced: Sweeney) was outraged to discover that the saint was founding a church on his land without his permission. Despite his wife Eorann's protestations, he attacked the church foundations, threw Rónán's psalter into a lake and was laying hands on the saint when a messenger arrived summoning Suibhne to the battlefield to assist an ally. When on the next day an otter returned the saint's psalter unharmed, Rónán gave thanks to heaven and cursed Suibhne.

What Suibhne saw in the battle (Mag Roth, in the year 637) drove him out of his mind: he took to the wilds, talked with animals and became bird-like, living in trees for seven years until his wits were restored. Finally, we are told, he 'died a Christian and his soul ascended to heaven'. There is a great deal of Celtic lore in this tale, and it hints at an on-going battle with the vestiges of pagan Druidism.

St Rónán of Iona is mentioned by Bede as arguing warmly with his countryman Fínán, bishop of Lindisfarne, over the Easter problem. Rónán supported the Roman dating of Easter, Fínán the

Celtic dating that the monks of Columba continued to use. At the Synod of Whitby in 664, the case was decided in favour of the Roman calculation.

To the left of the jetty, beyond the café and bar of the Martyr's Bay Restaurant, is the lovely **Port nam Mairtear**, as fitting a place as any to find the island's war memorial. At Martyr's Bay, in the year 806, sixty-eight monks of the monastery were slaughtered by Viking marauders. It was to this beautiful, fan-shaped bay that the corpses of kings and chieftains were carried across the sea, and the Street of the Dead starts at an Ealadh, the mound that stands at the head of the bay. If we ask ourselves why the bodies were first brought to Martyr's Bay, instead of one of the landing places closer to the burial ground, the answer may well lie with an Ealadh itself. 'Ealadh' signifies 'tomb', and specifically refers to this spot on Iona where the dead were placed upon landing. We know nothing about who might have been buried in this 'tomb'. If it was itself a place of burial, then we must assume that it houses a figure of some prominence, so that an Ealadh is a kind of 'Palladium': a source of protection. Here, the body of the king or lord was rested, and Lucy Menzies ('Saint Columba of Iona', 1920) states that the body was carried three times around the 'tomb' before progressing along the Sràid nam Marbh.

Iomair o, 'illean mhara,
'Illean o horo eile
Heave-ho, isle of the sea ...
Isle of the deep, in deep sleep dreaming,
Sails to thee a king a-sleeping,
With thy saints, into thy keeping ...
('Iona Boat Song')

Starting at an Ealadh, the old 'Street of the Dead' cut across the neighbouring field at a diagonal, passing in front of Dalantobair ('Field of the Well') and through what is now the Village Hall and the island's Library. The visitor today must join the old 'street' near the medical centre and the primary school by walking up the road from the jetty, past Iona Cottage on the left, and continuing in the direction of the Big Hill.

The Nunnery

Where the road turns sharply northwards stand the pretty ruins of the Benedictine Nunnery founded in 1203. The Nunnery, dedicated to St Mary the Virgin, was created by Reginald (or Ranald), Lord of the Isles, who installed his sister as its first prioress. Martin Martin in the 1690s read an inscribed stone in the ruined Nunnery which he claimed read: Behag Nijn Sorle vic Il vrid Priorissa ('Bethoc, Daughter to Somerled, son of Gillebride, Prioress'). Later, it became one of only two Augustinian orders of canonesses in Scotland. Women of noble birth were brought to Iona to be buried at the Nunnery right up until the mid eighteenth century.

The buildings clustered around the quadrangle known as the Cloister Garth, on the north side of which stood the Convent Church. The chancel of the church originally housed the gravestone effigy of Anna MacLean, the last Prioress, who died in 1543. The stone was broken when the rib-vaulted ceiling of the chancel collapsed in 1830, but an engraving of 1772 shows Anna with angels at her shoulders and lapdogs at her waist mirroring the lost section of the slab which depicts the Virgin and Child. The stone was later housed in Teampull Rónáin, St Ronan's Church, which adjoins the Nunnery. This small, plain chapel was the island's parish church from the beginning of the thirteenth century up until the Reformation, when astonishingly the island was left with no official place of worship until the Telford church was built in 1828 – a period of nearly three hundred years! When the floor of St Ronan's Church was excavated in 1992, remnants of a smaller and earlier chapel were discovered as well as burials that go back even further, suggesting a lay community on the island at the time of the early monastery.

To the east of the Cloister Garth stood the Chapter House with its stone benches, above which was the dormitory for the nuns (facing towards the Sound of Iona). The West Range (most of which stood where the modern road runs past the primary school) would have housed guests. The South Range was the refectory where the nuns took their meals. The buildings underwent some repair in 1923, when the garden was planted in the Cloister Garth in memory of Mrs R.J. Spencer. In relaying the floor of the church, workmen discovered three silver gilt spoons and a gold fillet or ornamental band wrapped in a fragment of cloth. The spoons dated from the twelfth or thirteenth centuries. Another fillet and a ring were discovered when the floor of St Ronan's was relaid in 1923.

The lovely ruins make a perfect place for rest and contemplation, especially in the low evening light as the sun, setting over Cnoc Mór, spreads a golden glow over the pink stones of the Nunnery and the pink rocks of Mull across the sea, and one can imagine angels clustering on the rocks across the Sound, beckoning to Columba, and the gentle voices of nuns, singing their orisons for three hundred years in this marvellous building which overlooks am Baile Mór – 'The Big Town'.

The Street of the Dead

Leaving the Nunnery grounds by the gate to the north of St Ronan's Chapel, we see to the left of us an attractive dell of deciduous trees between the primary school and the Iona Heritage Centre. This copse is all that remains of the woodland that once covered much of the island: from pollen studies we know that ash, birch, oak and willow existed on the isle in the time of Columba's monastery, and quite possibly hazel, as well as the likelihood of yew trees. The maps indicate one Cnoc Daraich or 'Oak Hill', to the north of the abbey, and Allt a' Chaorainn – 'Brook of the Rowan' – in the south, by **Uamh nan Calman**, 'Cave of the Pigeon, or Dove'.

The heritage centre was opened in 1990 inside the manse which was built to accompany the parish church of 1828. As well as offering a tea-room, the heritage centre displays many artefacts from Iona's past, particularly showing life on the island from 1770 onwards. "Yon neat trim church", as Wordsworth described the parish church, is one of a number commissioned by an Act of Parliament, passed in 1824, to provide new church buildings in the Highlands and Islands. These were based on a series of designs by the famed engineer Thomas Telford.

The road from the Nunnery to the Abbey passes, on the right-hand side, the Fraser Memorial. In 1979, the island (with the exception of the abbey buildings) was sold by the trustees of the 10th Duke of Argyll to the Fraser Foundation. The island was presented to the Scottish nation in memory of Lord Fraser of Allander. The Secretary of State for Scotland then handed ownership of the island to the National Trust for Scotland.

Continuing along the road, we briefly rejoin the Sràid nam Marbh by **MacLean's Cross**. This belongs to the fifteenth century and is a single shaft of schist, over three metres high, intricately carved on both sides. The west face depicts the crucifixion on the cross-head, the east (seaward) face being decorated with animals, foliage and Celtic plaitwork.

The modern road sweeps up past the parish church and onwards, between the St Columba Hotel (formerly the Free Church manse) and the tiny Iona Bookshop, which sells second-hand and antiquarian volumes, before we come to St Oran's Chapel and Iona's famous royal burial ground.

Reilig Odhráin

The Irish 'Life of Columcille', dating from the mid twelfth century, first refers to "Odhran laid in earth on I-Columcille". We have seen in the previous section that "Odhran of Iona, of severe piety" is mentioned in 'The Book of Ballymote'. In the curious legend of the burial of Oran we are told that Columba assured his friend that, "No one will be granted his request at my own grave, unless he first seek it of you" – in other words, that Columba's sacred precinct would be approached via the grave of Oran.

Donald Munro, Archdeacon of the Isles, visited Iona and wrote in his 'Description of the Western Isles' of 1549:

"Within the ile of Colmkill, there is ane sanctuary also, or kirkzaird, callit in Erische Religoran quhilk is a very fair Kirkzaird and weill biggit about with staine and lyme. Into this sanctuary there is three tombes of staine formit like little chapels, with ane braid gray marble or quhin staine in the gavill of ilk ane of the tombes. In the staine of the ane tombe there is written in Latin letters, Tumulus Regum Scotiae, that is the tombe ore grave of the Scotts Kinges: within this tombe according to our Scotts and Erische cronikels ther layes fortey-eight crouned Scotts Kinges. The tombe on the South side forsaid hes this inscription, Tumulus Regum Hyberniae, that is the tombe of the Irland Kinges – there was foure Irland Kinges eirdit in the said tombe. Upon the north side of ane Scotts tombe, the inscriptione beares Tumulus Regum Norwegiae, that is the tombe of the Kings of Norroway – ther layes eight Kings of Norroway ... because it was the maist honorable and ancient place that was in Scotland in thair dayes."

He went on to mention the Lords of the Isles buried there, along with "sundrie uther inhabitants of the haille isles."

By 1772, the traveller Thomas Pennant was to write: "Of these celebrated tombs we could discover nothing more than certain slight remains, that were built in a ridged form, and arched within: but the inscriptions were lost."

The poet Keats, visiting in the summer of 1818, wrote to his brother in London:

"We were shown a spot in the Churchyard where they say 61 Kings are buried 48 Scotch from Fergus 2nd to Mackbeth 8 Irish 4 Norwegian and 1 french – they lie in rows compact. Then we were shown other matters of interest of later date but still very ancient – many tombs of Highland Chieftains – their effigies in complete armour face upwards – black and moss covered – Abbots and Bishops of the island always of one of the chief Clans. There were plenty Macleans and Macdonnels, among these latter the famous Macdonel Lord of the Isles".

From the existing records we can state with some certainty that the following kings and chiefs lie buried here:

Ecgfrith, King of Northumberland, who died on Saturday 20th May, 685, at the battle of Nechtansmere. Riagal of Bangor wrote of his death: "Although he did penance, he shall lie in Hi after his death". Both Ecgfrith's father and uncle had taken sanctuary on Iona in 616 during their exile from Northumbria, which might ease the fact that the earliest substantiated burial on Iona belongs to a king who died warring against the Picts, the Britons and the Scots of Dalriada.

Bruide mac Bili, King of the Picts, who died circa 692. A remarkable figure, whose original power base was amongst the Maeatae, against whom Artuir mac Áedán died fighting. He extended his territory northwards to the Orkneys, westwards to Kintyre and southwards into the region controlled by Northumbria. He was a friend of Adomnán, who stood vigil over his body until it began to open its eyes, at which point a monk came to the door and said, "If Adomnán's object be to raise the dead, I say he should not do so, for it will be a degradation to every cleric who shall succeed in his place, if he too cannot raise the dead." Adomnán took the hint and blessed the body and soul of his friend, King Bruide. He also composed an elegy which ends –

> Is annamh,
> iar mbeith i rríghe thuaithe,
> ceppán caue crínn dara
> im mac rígh Ala Cluaithi.
>
> "It is rare (strange),
> after being the king of a people:
> a small ruined stump of oak
> about the son of the king of Dumbarton."

Niall Frossach, King of Ireland, who died in 778. The son of Fergal, Niall gained his nickname, 'The Showery', after the omens surrounding his birth, which were translated by the bards into 'A shower of silver, a shower of wheat and a shower of honey.' He became high king at Tara in 763, and ruled for seven years before taking holy orders. He lived out the last eight years of his life as a monk on Iona.

Artgal, King of Connaught, who reigned for five years before spending the last eight years of his life as a monk on Iona, dying there in 791.

Kenneth mac Alpin, King of Scots, who died of a tumour in February, 858. Described as 'The Slayer' in the Prophecy of Berchan, Kenneth's rise to power was swift and bloody, and helped by an alliance with the Viking chief of the 'Isles of the Strangers', as the Hebrides were then known. Kenneth rebuilt the church at Dunkeld, gifting it with relics of St Columba brought from Iona in 849. The Scottish 'Chronicle of the Kings' states that he was "buried in the island of Iona, where the three sons of Erc were buried."

Donald mac Alpin, King of Scots and half-brother of Kenneth, "assassinated at Scone" in 862.

Constantine I, King of Scots, son of Kenneth mac Alpin. His sister was married to Olaf, the Viking warlord of Dublin, and the fact that Constantine ruled for sixteen years must largely be due to his alliance with the Norseman. However, it was the Viking warriors of Halfdan ('the Black') Ivarsson that clashed with the "men of Alba" on the shore of Inverdovat, and there perished Constantine I in 877.

Aed, King of Scots, son of Kenneth mac Alpin, who reigned for at most a year, and was slain near Strathallan in 878 by his cousin's warband.

Giric, King of Scots, who ruled jointly with Eochaid, the last British king of Strathclyde, a grandson of both Artgal and Kenneth. Giric, son of Donald mac Alpin, died in 889.

Donald II, King of Scots, son of Constantine. Deposed his cousins Giric and Eochaid and was the first to be described as Rí Albain, or King of Scotland. Donald died at Forres in the year 900.

Malcolm I, King of Scots, son of Donald. The name Malcolm derives from the Gaelic Máel Coluim, meaning 'follower of Columba'. He succeeded to the throne on the abdication of Constantine II, who died a monk at St Andrews in 943. Malcolm was slain at the battle of Fetteresso in 954.

Induif, King of Scots, son of Constantine II, who reigned for nine years and was killed by Norsemen in 962.

Dubh, King of Scots, son of Malcolm. Slain by a rival claimant to the throne at Forres in 966. The 'Chronicle of the Kings' tells us that his body was "hidden away under the bridge of Kinloss. But the sun did not appear so long as he was concealed there; and he was found, and buried in the island of Iona."

Olav Sitricsson, King of Dublin and York, who died in 981. Also known as Olav Cuaran: 'Olav the Sandal'. Firstly, he was king of Jorvik, but was expelled on his conversion to Christianity. He became king of Dublin, reclaiming York after the expulsion of Erik Bloodaxe but losing it again three years later. After the battle of Tara, Olav "went to Iona in penitence and pilgrimage". Therefore, a Viking king who had plundered the monastery at Kells, where the monks of Iona had taken refuge for over 150 years, himself became a royal monk on Iona.

Kenneth II, King of Scots, son of Malcolm. He reigned for twenty-four years, from 971 till 995, when he was killed "by trickery and craft" in a conspiracy engineered by Constantine the Bald, the grandson of Indulf, and Giric, the grandson of Dubh.

Constantine III, King of Scots. Constantine 'the Bald' reigned for just eighteen months before he was killed by Kenneth, grandson of Malcolm, in 997.

Giric II, King of Scots, who ruled with his father Kenneth. Both were slain after eight years in battle at 'the moor of the bards' in 1005.

Malcolm II, King of Scots, son of Kenneth II. The 'Aggressor' and "honour of all the west of Europe", according to the 'Annals of Tigernach'. The last remaining male heir of Kenneth Mac Alpin died an old man, at Glamis, on the 25th November, 1034.

Duncan "The Gracious", King of Scots, grandson of Malcolm II. Despite Shakespeare's description of him –

"... this Duncan
Hath borne his faculties so meek, hath been
So clear in his great office, that his virtues
Will plead like angels, trumpet-tongu'd, against
The deep damnation of his taking-off ..."

he was, at best, an unlucky king whose force was routed when he besieged Durham in 1039, and in the following year he was killed in battle near Elgin by Macbeth.

Macbeth, King of Scots, second husband of Gruoch, granddaughter of Kenneth III who had ruled jointly with his son Giric till he was killed by Malcolm II in 1005. In contrast to his Shakespearean portrait, Macbeth was a popular, generous ruler. The Prophecy of Berchan describes him as 'The Red King': "Scotland will be brimful, in the west and in the east, during the reign of the furious Red One." During his pilgrimage to Rome in 1050, the 'Anglo-Saxon Chronicle' speaks of him "scattering money like seed". He was finally slain in battle at Lumphanan in Mar by Duncan's son Malcolm, on the 15th August 1057, seventeen years to the day after he had defeated Duncan.

Lulach, King of Scots, who died in 1058. Known as Lulach Fatuus, Lulach 'the Fool' was the son of Gruoch by her first marriage. He reigned a mere four months before he was tracked down and killed by Malcolm III, otherwise known as Malcolm Canmore (Ceann Mór: 'Great Chieftain' or 'Big Head')

Donald III, King of Scots, son of Duncan I. When Malcolm had fled to Northumberland after their father's death at the hands of Macbeth, Donald went to the Hebrides. As Domnall Bàn, 'Donald the Fair', he assumed the Scottish throne on the death of Malcolm Canmore, but was expelled after six months by the Norman invasion force that briefly established **Duncan II**, son of Malcolm, on the throne. Already in his sixties, he returned to power for three years after Duncan's death, until he was tortured and executed by Edgar, son of Queen Margaret, at the head of another English invasion. Buried first at Dunkeld, his remains were reburied on Iona early in the twelfth century.

The annals mention two more kings – **Godred Olavsson**, King of Man and the Isles, and **Upsak 'Haakon'**, King of the Isles – as being buried on Columba's isle. Godred died on the 10th November 1187 on St Patrick's Island off the shore of the Isle of Man. The 'Chronicle of Man' tells us that, in the following summer, "his body was removed to the Island called Iona". Upsak, a grandson of the mighty Somerled, was despatched in the year 1230 by the King of Norway to bring order to the Hebrides. In besieging the Isle of Bute, Upsak was struck by a rock thrown from the castle walls. Twenty-one years earlier, we are told, Upsak went "a-viking west-over-sea" and pillaged the holy island. Upsak now returned to that holy island as the last king to be buried in its hallowed soil.

After the kings came the Lords of the Isles, a dynasty founded by **Somerled**, whose name means 'Summer Voyager', and whose father was the exiled King of Argyll, Gillebride, or 'Servant of Bride'. Somerled married Ragnild, daughter of Olav the Red, King of Man, and raised Argyll against Olav's son Godred, defeating the Viking battle fleet off the coast of Islay on the 6th January 1156.

It was probably Somerled who commissioned the rebuilding of St Oran's as a family burial chapel. Somerled died in 1164. Malcolm IV, King of Scotland from 1153 to 1165, "sent a boat with the corpse of Somerled to Icolumkill at his own charges", although it seems that Somerled was later reburied at the priory of Saddell on Kintyre.

His son, Reginald or **Ranald**, founded "a monastery of Black Monks in Iona, in honour of God and Columcille" and "a monastery of Black Nuns in the same place". The 'Book of Clanranald' tells us that "He died and was buried at Reilig Odhráin in Iona in the year of our Lord 1207." His son and heir was the pirate **Donald of Islay**, founder of the Clan Donald, who died in 1249 and was buried on Iona, as was his son **Angus Mór** ('Angus the Great') who died on Islay in 1292.

Angus Òg – Angus the Young – fought alongside Robert the Bruce at Bannockburn in 1314. He was buried in the Teampull Odhráin (St Oran's Chapel), his intricately carved gravestone bearing the galley symbol of Clan Donald. He is the hero of Sir Walter Scott's 'Lord of the Isles' – "The heir of mighty Somerled ... The fair, the valiant and the young ..."

The first Lord of the Isles to be so called was **John of Islay**: "... his fair body was brought to Iona of Columcille, and the abbot and the monks and vicars came to meet him ... and his service and waking were honourably performed during eight days and eight nights, and he was laid in the same grave with his father in Teampull Odhrain in the year of our Lord 1380." ('Book of Clanranald')

Donald of Harlaw, son of John of Islay, was the next Lord of the Isles. After the bloody and inconclusive battle of Harlaw (1411), in which he fought to claim the Earldom of Ross on behalf of his wife Mairi, Donald seems to have devoted himself to spiritual matters, giving lands to the monastery of Iona and making a covering of gold and silver for the relic of the hand of Columba. His "full noble body" was buried on the south side of St Oran's Chapel.

No more Lords of the Isles were buried here – indeed, Donald's grandson John surrendered the Lordship to James IV of Scotland and died in poverty at Dundee.

The twelve chieftains who together composed the Council of the Isles each had a claim to a tomb in Reilig Odhráin. Martin Martin refers to a "Heap of Stones without the Church under which Mackean of Ardnamurchan lies buried." He also mentions a "Tomb of Gilbrid" – possibly the father of Somerled – and notes that "The families of Mack-Lean of Duart, Loch-buy, and Coll, lie next all in Armour, as big as the Life."

Red Hector Maclean of Duart, who died fighting for Donald, Lord of the Isles, at Harlaw, shares a grave with **Sallow Hector**, ninth chief of the Macleans of Duart, who died beside James IV at the battle of Flodden Field in 1513.

Among those buried more recently in Reilig Odhráin are the crew and passengers of the **Guy Mannering**, a 'packet' ship that sailed between Liverpool and New York during the American

Civil War. She was wrecked within a quarter of a mile of the beach of the Bay at the Back of the Ocean – and, on the 31st December 1865, the 32 crew and six passengers abandoned ship and attempted to swim for shore, where the islanders, linking arms and venturing out into the waves, struggled to save them. Seventeen perished. A monument was erected by the United States in the graveyard.

In the 1990s, the graveyard was extended to the north-east, and it is here, under a simple stone, that **John Smith**, Leader of the Labour Party, was laid to rest in 1994.

St Oran's Chapel is the oldest remaining building on the island – it is also one of the oldest ecclesiastical buildings in Scotland. It was first restored by Queen (later, Saint) Margaret, wife of Malcolm Canmore. They visited the island in about 1072 and "the Queen restored the smaller church of Columcille". The restoration was therefore started by a Hungarian-born English princess who hated both the Gaelic language and the Celtic Church. She was a Romanist through and through, and with her husband the tradition of burying the Kings of Scotland on Iona ended. Margaret died of grief four days after Malcolm was killed in an ambush in Northumberland: both are buried at Dunfermline.

The chapel was last restored in 1957 and presents itself as a beautifully simple oratory where services can still be held. A late fifteenth century tomb recess adorns the inside wall, but otherwise St Oran's Chapel is without interior decoration and is all the more spiritual for it. There is no electricity or gas – just candles and prayers and the souls of the noble dead of many centuries.

In the field between St Oran's and the sea, at the edge of the old abbey vallum can been seen the remains of the thirteenth century Caibeal Muire – 'St Mary's Chapel'.

The Abbey

Entering the abbey grounds from the south-west, the pathway runs between an excavated stretch of the late medieval Street of the Dead and **Tòrr Abb** – the 'Abbot's Mound' – referred to by Martin Martin as Dùn nam Manach. Columba was reckoned to have a writing hut on this hill, where in later years a medieval cross stood. It is also a contender for the hill, mentioned by Adomnán in his 'Life of St Columba', which overlooked the monastery and which the saint climbed shortly before his death, raising his hands to bless the monastery and saying:

"This place, however small and mean, will have bestowed on it no small but great honour by the kings and peoples of Ireland, and also by the rulers of even barbarous and foreign nations with their subject tribes. And the saints of others churches too will give it great reverence."

Three great crosses stand before the abbey. **St Martin's Cross** is the only one that remains complete. The whinstone shaft was brought over from the mainland in the second half of the eighth century. It is set in a pedestal of granite. The side facing the visitor is decorated with ornamental bosses and serpent designs; the east side (facing the abbey) depicts a range of Biblical subjects, included David playing the harp, Abraham about to sacrifice Isaac, Daniel with a pair of lions, and a centre-piece of the Virgin and Child surrounded by angels. A faint inscription in Irish letters, uncovered in 1927, read: "A prayer for Gilla Christ who made this cross".

St Martin of Tours founded the monastic system in the fourth century. St Ninian, who was said to be related to St Martin, brought the ideal to Galloway in Scotland, there establishing his Candida Casa, later known as Whithorn, in about 397. St Finnian of Moville, future teacher of Columba, trained there, and with Columba the system was transplanted to Iona.

The broken shaft of **St Matthew's Cross** stands before the entrance to the abbey church, near the medieval well. The front side shows the 'Temptation', but otherwise little can be made out of the cross's design. To the left, standing in front of St Columba's Shrine, is a replica of **St John's Cross**.

Immediately behind St John's Cross is the tiny stone chapel known as **St Columba's Shrine**, which may date back to the ninth century. Adomnán refers to Columba's burial place only as having for its memorial the stone he used for a pillow. His remains were supposedly enshrined in a silver casket or reliquary. In 825, Viking raiders, who had already slaughtered a number of monks, broke into the chapel where the abbot Blathmac was celebrating mass. They demanded the precious reliquary, but Blathmac refused to impart its whereabouts, so they killed him there and then. The shockwaves from this savage assault rippled across Europe: Walahfrid Strabo, a monk at the monastery of Reichenau in southern Germany, wrote a poem bewailing the event.

In the 'Leabhar Breac', St Brechan remarks of Columba:

His grace in Hii without stain,
And his soul in Derry;
And his body under the flagstone
Under which are Brigid and Patrick.

This would refer to the ancient church in Down that Lord Grey, Deputy Governor of Ireland, 1536-7, put to the flame in his eagerness to carry out Henry the Eighth's policies. The historian Holinshed tells us: "He rode to the north and in his journey he razed St. Patrick, his church in Downe, and burnt the monuments of Patrick, Brigide and Colme, who are said to have been there interred." Lord Grey was eventually tried and executed on Tower Hill in London in 1541.

The islanders continued vigorously to insist that the saint's remains never left Iona. Father Thomas Innes wrote, early in the eighteenth century, that: "It is the constant tradition and belief of the inhabitants of Ycolmkill and of the neighbourhood at this day that St Columba's body lies still in this island, being hidden by pious people at the time of the new Reformation, in some secure and private place in or about the church, as it used frequently to be in former times during the ravages of the infidel Danes."

Possibly, the shrine was erected on the site of the original grave. One wonders whether it was this "small church of Columcille" or the "smaller church of Columchille" – St Oran's, restored by Queen Margaret in 1072 – that Magnus Barelegs visited in 1098. The Norwegian King had adopted the kilt after his time spent in the Hebrides. Although he wished to open the "small church", the king did not go in, "but closed the door again immediately, and immediately locked it, and said that none should be so daring as to go into that church; and thenceforward it has been so done." Magnus instead sailed to Islay for his plunder and pillage.

The **Nave** of the church was rebuilt in 1910. The west entrance brings the visitor under five attractive west-facing windows into the Church of St Mary. Hard to the right are glass cases displaying a facsimile of the **Book of Kells**, a Celtic treasure believed to have been written and illuminated by the monks of Iona before being transferred to Kells, in County Meath, for safekeeping. The skins of some 185 calves were used in creating this beautiful volume which is now kept at Trinity College, Dublin.

Much of the **North Transept**, restored in 1904, dates back to the Benedictine church established by Ranald mac Somerled around 1200. The **Crossing** with its two-storeyed tower containing a belfry and medieval pigeon-loft, belongs mainly to the fifteenth century.

On the 14th March, 1635, King Charles I wrote to the Bishop of Raphoe demanding that two of the bells that had been taken by Bishop Knox from the bishopric of the Isles, "without just cause or aney warrant frome our late royall father or us", be returned to the Cathedral Church of Iona. In that same year, Charles I also wrote to the Lords of the Exchequer requiring "the sume of Fower hundred pounds Sterlin" to be granted to the Bishop of the Isles "to repayre the Cathedrall Church of Icolmkill". This scheme appears to have been forestalled by the political upheavals which led to the English Civil War, and no restoration work was carried out until the beginning of the twentieth century.

The oak-screen in the crossing arch was a gift from Queen Elizabeth II in 1956. The **South Transept** is dominated by the marble effigy of George, Eighth Duke of Argyll, who granted the abbey ruins to the Iona Cathedral Trust in 1899 on condition that they restored the buildings for worship. He died in the following year. Beside him lies his third wife, Ina McNeill, who was buried in the church in 1925. On the 14th July 1905, the first service was held in the partially-restored church.

The **Choir** shows the most amount of rebuilding over the centuries, including the remains of a **South East Transept** on the outside of the **South Aisle**. Much of this was laid out in the fifteenth century to cater for the increasing number of pilgrims passing through the church. It may have been the master-mason from this period of construction who carved his name in Lombardic letters on the south-east capital of the Tower Crossing: "DONALDUS O BROLCHAN FECIT HOC OPUS" – 'Donald Ó Brolchan made this work'.

The twentieth century communion table is carved from Iona marble, quarried on the island, replacing the original high altar which fell victim to souvenir hunters in the eighteenth century. On the wall to the right of the communion table can be seen a carved cat and monkey. In front of the altar lie the stone effigies of Abbot John MacKinnon (who died around 1500) and Abbot Dominic (1421 – circa 1465) who together oversaw much of the fifteenth century rebuilding.

Three pointed arches open into the south aisle of the choir. The arches are decorated with a variety of carvings, including contemporary scenes of soldiers, armed riders and a cow being slaughtered. Four twentieth century stained glass windows show St Patrick, St Brigid, St Margaret of Scotland (Queen Margaret) and St Columba.

The delightful quadrangle of the abbey **Cloister** was restored in the late 1950s using some of the original decorated columns. Around the walls stand samples of West Highland gravestones commemorating "the best men of all the Isles", most of them removed from Reilig Odhráin after being uncovered by the Iona Club in 1833. In the centre of the lawn stands a bronze sculpture by

Jacques Lipchtiz depicting 'The Descent of the Spirit' in the form of a dove (Columba = 'dove'). The abbey gift shop is reached through a low doorway in the north-west corner of the cloister garth. The **Refectory**, restored in 1949, occupied the second storey of the **North Range**, above the gift shop. Here the monks took their meals while the abbot read Biblical texts from a pulpit in the north wall.

Unlike the **West Range** of 1965, which is completely modern, the **East Range** (restored 1956) contained the chapter house, where the monks met to discuss their daily business, and above that the dormitory. A night-stair led from the dormitory to the north transept giving the monks access to the church for nocturnal services. The library above the chapter house was restored in 1940 in memory of Alexander and Euphemia Ritchie, curators of the abbey buildings, whose 'Iona Past and Present' (1928) preserved many of the island's place-names as well as detailing its floral and fauna. Of the original library, Thomas Pennant in 'Voyage to the Hebrides' (1772) referred to Hector Boece's claim that Fergus II brought a chest of books to Iona from his plunder of Rome in 410, and that Aeneas Sylvius – later Pope Pius II – hoped to find the lost books of Livy there before the death of King James I deprived him of the opportunity. The monastery's written records and other valuables were destroyed by the Synod and the earl of Argyll in 1642.

North of the refectory stands the **Abbot's House**, connected to the **Reredorter**, or latrine, which was drained using water channelled from the Mill Stream. Both of these buildings were restored in the 1950s. The remains of Tigh an Easbuig – 'House of the Bishop' – stand in the field beyond the stream, and perhaps date from the 1630s when the abbey church was briefly the Cathedral of the Isles. The area around Buidhneach, signifying 'numerous' or 'in companies' and usually translated as the 'Place of Yellow Flowers', is also known as the **Bishop's Walk**, between Dùn Ì and the north road.

Beyond the reredorter building is the **Infirmary**, now a museum housing carved stones from the abbey and the nunnery. These include the remnants of the St John's and St Oran's crosses, both dating from the eighth century, as well as a wealth of early Christian and Norse gravestones.

A few metres from the infirmary museum stands the **Michael Chapel**. This chapel dates back to the thirteenth century and might have been the main place of worship while the abbey was being built. A simple, almost sombre chamber, its African timbers bear witness to the African donations that financed the restoration of 1961.

Returning to the front of the abbey, we should pause at the **Peace Garden**, planted in the ruins of the abbey's bakery and brewery, where the Street of the Dead reaches its end.

In 1938, the Iona Community was established by Dr George MacLeod – later the Very Reverend Lord MacLeod of Fuinary – minister of Govan Old Parish Church in Glasgow. The community was a Church of Scotland brotherhood whose aims were to bring volunteers to help with the rebuilding of the abbey and to train young ministers for working in difficult inner city areas. Volunteers arrive every year to live and work at the abbey, in the Iona Community Shop across the road, and at the MacLeod Centre which lies up the track between the shop and Burnside Cottage. The community tends the herb beds north of the old bakehouse and the Peace Garden itself. Here, the visitor sits at the very hub of the abbey grounds, safe within the kidney-shaped vallum or defensive rampart that might pre-date the Christian monastery. A breeze blows in from the sea and the flowers nod their heads in the sun. This is the sacred heart of the Isle of the Saints.

Saint Columba

In sermone suo siluit ventus.
Et cogitatione sua placavit abissum.

For his sermon the wind was still.
And by his thoughts he calmed the deep.
(Versicle and Response from the
Lauds for the Feast of St Columba)

Columba was born at Gartan, County Donegal, in the year 521 – possibly on the 7th December, a Thursday – by tradition, a lucky day:

Thursday of Columba benign,
Day to send sheep on prosperity,
Day to send cow on calf,
Day to put the web in the warp.

Day to put coracle on the brine,
Day to place the staff to the flag,
Day to bear, day to die,
Day to hunt the heights.

Day to put horses in harness,
Day to send herds to pasture,
Day to make prayer efficacious,
Day of my beloved, the Thursday.
(Carmina Gadelica)

Both St Brigid and St Patrick had foreseen his coming. His mother Eithne, of the ruling house of Leinster, had dreamt of an angel bearing a cloth "in which the most beautiful colours of all the flowers seemed to be portrayed". In her dream she saw that "its measurement was larger than mountains or forests". This cloth was her future son.

His father was Fedilmid, son of Fergus, son of Conall, son of Niall Noígiallach – the legendary Niall of the Nine Hostages, founder of the Uí Néill, the ruling dynasties of Ireland. Had he not become a missionary, Columba might have become Ireland's king.

Tradition states that his birth name was Crimthann, a name variously translated as 'fox' or 'wolf', but at his baptism he took the name Columb, meaning 'dove'. In time to come, he would be known as 'Columcille', Dove of the Church.

At an early age, Columba was fostered with the priest Cruithnechán who had officiated at his baptism. Later, he was sent to the monastic school of Moville, where he studied under St

Finnian. He went next to Leinster, to learn under the Christian bard known as Gemmán, where his love of poetry was embedded, before receiving his final monastic training at Clonard at the source of the river Boyne, under another St Finnian. Columba's fellow students at Clonard included Ciaran of Clonmacnoise and Brendan of Clonfert, who set out on an epic seven-year sea journey to find the Land of Promise. When Columba left Clonard he was an ordained priest.

At about the age of twenty-five, he founded the first of the thirty-seven monasteries he is reputed to have established in Ireland alone. Derry – the 'Place of the Oaks' – was the site, and Columba exhibited a druidical reverence for the oak tree, refusing to see one felled in the construction of his church:

> I love my beautiful Derry
> For its quietness and its purity,
> For heaven's angels that come and go,
> Under every leaf of the oaks,
> I love my beautiful Derry.
> My Derry, my fair oak-grove ...

Another monastery of Columba's was also associated with oak trees: Durrow – the 'Plain of the Oaks'. Monasteries at Raphoe, Drumhone, Sords and Kells followed. These activities occupied Columba for fifteen years, until the turning point of his life came at the battle of Cúl Drebene.

It all started when Finnian of Moville returned from Rome bearing sacred books given to him by Pope Pelagius. Not only was Columba eager to see the St Jerome translation of the Scriptures; he decided to make a copy for himself and so remained in the church after services, copying the Psalter out in his own hand over twelve nights. We are told that "the fingers of his right hand were as candles which shone like five very bright lamps". A messenger, sent to fetch the Psalter from the church, spied on Columba through a hole in the door. Columba, who kept a pet crane beside him, bade the bird peck out the boy's eye, "who came to observe me without my knowledge". Finnian put right the damage to the messenger's eye, and the two clergymen took their dispute to Diarmait, High King of Ireland, at Tara.

Finnian complained that Columba had transcribed the book without permission and that, therefore, the transcript belonged to Finnian. Columba countered that he had deprived his old tutor of nothing – rather he was seeking to promote the Gospel.

Diarmait deliberated, and finally gave his judgement:

"To every cow her calf, to every book its copy." The transcript belonged to Finnian.

Columba swore that Diarmait's judgement was wrong, but to make matters worse, a youth who had inadvertently killed another during a game of hurley ran to Columba for protection. Diarmait's men dragged the boy away and put him to death on the spot.

Columba made his way home to his own people, composing on the mountain road his 'Song of Trust':

> Better is He in whom we trust,
> The King who has made us all,
> Who will not leave me tonight without refuge.
> I adore not the voice of birds,
> Nor chance, nor the love of a son or a wife,
> My Druid is Christ, the Son of God.

So the Cenél Conaill and Cenél nÉogain rose up against their supreme ruler.

On the night before the battle, the Archangel Michael appeared to Columba, informing him that his side would be victorious, but his penance would be to exile himself from Ireland. On the day itself, Diarmait marched his forces thrice round a cairn sunwise while his Druids raised an airbhe – a 'ghost fence' or supernatural mist – which no enemy could cross. The Archangel Michael was seen to lead Columba's host. Three thousand men died that day, but only one from Columba's side. Diarmait was defeated. The book, which had sparked the trouble, was set in a silver shrine and ever more was carried before the host of the Cenél Conaill to guarantee them victory.

At a synod held at Teltown in Meath, Columba was excommunicated in absentia. He appealed, and his sentence was commuted to the task of winning as many souls for Christ as had died that day at Cúl Debrene.

Thus, Columba and twelve companions set forth from Ireland in a curragh, a large coracle formed of stout branches wrapped with hides. Columba's boat was called "Dewy-Red", and it sailed from Loch Foyle in the year 563.

Dál Riata

The Scotti, who came from a district of Antrim in Northern Ireland, and the Epidii – the Celtic tribe of Argyll – had been engaged in trade, probably for centuries. In Irish myth, the beautiful Deirdre of the Sorrows fled from Ireland to Argyll with the sons of Uisneach to avoid the lecherous advances of the ageing King Conchobar. This exodus, which brought the Druids of Nechtan across from Ireland, may have happened as early as the first century. Europe's second largest whirlpool, Corryvreckan, between the isles of Scarba and Jura, derives from Coire Breccáin, the 'Cauldron of Breccán'. Breccán mac Máine maic Néill plied the trade route between Ireland and Scotland until his fifty coracles were lost in the maelstrom.

Sometime around the year 220, the Scots began to colonise the region we now know as 'Argyll', which means '(East) Margin of the Strangers'. The colony took its name from its home in Ireland: Dál Riata.

In the year 498, three sons of the Dalriadic King Erc sailed to Scotland to establish themselves as rulers of the colony. Fergus Mór, the eldest, took as his seat the hill-fort at Dunadd, in Kintyre. Loarn based himself at Dunollie, near Oban (visible from the ferry crossing to Mull) and governed the area known as the Firth of Lorne. Oengus took Islay in the west. Under this triumvirate, Dál Riata became a kingdom.

Fergus Mór did not last long. The 'Annals of Tigernach' enter his obituary for the year 501. Neither, it seems, did his son Domangart, who reigned for six years, siring two sons: Gabrán and Comgall. Gabrán died in 559, and it was after him that the ruling Kintyre branch of Dál Riata – the Cenél nGabráin – was named. Loarn founded the northern branch, the Cenél Loairn, and Oengus the Cenél nOenguso in Islay. All three sons of Erc were buried on Iona, so tradition has it, indicating that Iona was already the holy island of Dál Riata by the start of the sixth century.

Columba's grandmother was said to have been a daughter of Erc and sister to Fergus Mór. Tradition sites the grave of Columba's mother, Eithne, at Eilean an Naoimh – or 'Isle of the Saints' – in the Firth of Lorne, where Brendan of Clonfert founded a settlement before Columba came to Iona.

From 559, the king of Dál Riata was Conall mac Comgaill. It was to King Conall's stronghold in Kintyre that Columba and his followers first sailed. Adomnán tells us that Columba described to Conall a battle that was just then taking place in Ireland: this was "two years after the battle of Cúl Debrene, when the holy man first set sail from Ireland to be a pilgrim".

It seems that roundabout the time of Gabrán's death, the Picts under their king Bruide began to fight back against the encroachments of the Scots. Parts of Dál Riata were reclaimed by Pictland and may not have been won back for Dál Riata until about the time of Conall's death (574). Adomnán tells us that Columba favoured Éogenán mac Gabráin for the succession – suggesting that he was the next in line – and yet an angel appeared to St Columba in a vision over three nights, bearing "a glass book of the ordination of kings" and striking Columba across the cheek, commanding him to ordain Áedán. A mere fourteen years earlier, King Diarmait of Ireland had celebrated a pagan ritual in which the king 'slept with' the goddess of sovereignty during his ordination at Tara. Columba's dream or vision is a Christian version of the pagan Tarbfeis which 'dreamt' the next king in succession.

Columba duly crowned Áedán mac Gabráin King of Dál Riata on Iona in 574, opening up a thirty year period of warfare between the Dalriadic Scots, the Welsh-speaking Britons, the Picts and the Saxons of northern England. The battle against the Miathi, or Maeatae, near Stirling was 'seen' by Columba on Iona: "Now the barbarians are turned in flight and victory is granted to Áedán, though it is not a happy one." It was this battle, circa 590, that cost Áedán his son, Artuir, or Arthur of Dál Riata. Finally, Áedán was heavily defeated by the Northumbrian king Aethelfrith at the battle of Degastan (in Dumfriesshire) in 603.

In about 565, Columba set off to negotiate with Bruide, son of Maelchon (or Maelgwyn), king of the Picts. This entailed a journey to Inverness, and the first recorded mention of a 'water beast' in Loch Ness, with which Columba dealt summarily. Adomnán mentions several contests with the wizards (Druids) of the Pictish king. Manus O'Donnell, writing his 'Life of St Columba' in 1532, tells us that on his arrival at Iona, Columba was approached by two 'Bishops' of the island who "came to lead Columba by the hand out of it. But God revealed to Colum Cille that they were not true Bishops, whereupon they left the island to him when he told them of their history and their true adventures". The 'Martyrology of Oengus the Culdee' refers to the "seven bishops of Hii" and the church of Columba did not include bishops, so this may refer to an earlier Christian settlement sacred to the kings of Dál Riata.

We can surmise that by 500, Iona was established as the sacred isle (and burial place) of the kings of Dál Riata, of whom there were said to have been thirty before Kenneth mac Alpin which, added to the eighteen royal Scottish burials on record, makes up the 'fortey-eight crouned Scotts Kinges' mentioned by Munro in 1549. Around the year 560, however, the Picts fought back, possibly reclaiming Iona and re-establishing a form of Druidism. In 563, Columba sailed from Ireland, visiting his cousin King Conall who gave Iona to Columba "as an offering". The Venerable Bede, in his 'Ecclesiastical History of the English People', tells us that "Columba arrived in Britain in the ninth year of the reign of the powerful Pictish king, Bride son of Meilochon; he converted that people to the Faith of Christ by his preaching and example, and received from them the island of Iona on which to found a monastery." It could be said that Columba first gained his royal cousin's sanction to kick the Pictish Druids out, and then sought permission from the Pictish king to stay there.

I Columb Chille

"How swift is the speed of my coracle,
Its stern toward Derry;
I grieve at my errand over the noble sea,
Travelling to Alba of the ravens,
My foot in my dear little coracle,
My heart still bleeding."
(Columba's Farewell to Ireland)

On the southern shore of Iona there lies a pebbly beach, overlooked by Dùn Làthraichean, the 'Fort of the Ruins, or Sites', where the remains of circular dwellings – possibly pre-Christian – nestle on a plateau above 'Easter Cave'. This stony beach is **Port a' Churaich**, the 'Port of the Coracle', where tradition holds that Columba and his companions landed on the 12th May, the eve of Whitsunday, 563.

A raised mound, some sixty feet long, stands at the head of the bay in Glac a' Chulaidh, the 'Hollow of the Boat'. Here the companions of Columba are said to have buried their curragh in an act not unlike that of Cortez burning his boats on arrival in the New World. Given their reliance on sea-transport, this burial of their vessel seems unlikely. Columba is also supposed to have climbed the high point, Druim an Aoinidh, the 'Ridge of the Cliff', on the south-west corner of the island. A pile of stones – **Carn Cùl ri Eirinn**, the 'Cairn of the Back to Ireland' – marks the spot where the saint gazed south and found that his native land could no longer be seen.

Columba was forty-two years old. His voice was "so loud and melodious that it could be heard a mile away ... yet sweet with more than the sweetness of the bards". For the remaining thirty-four years of his life we would be based on Iona, writing, praying, building his community and preaching to the people of 'Alba of the ravens', perhaps so called because they still clung to the Druidic practice of divination through 'raven-knowledge'.

In The Dream of Rhonabwy from the Welsh 'mabinogion' we read of a game of chess played between Arthur and Owein, "son of Uryen". King Urien of North Rheged was assassinated in 590 by a jealous ally in the North British Alliance; it is likely that Artuir ('Arthur') fell in battle against the southern Picts in that same year. Owein, son of Urien, held the British kingdom for just another few years before dying in battle.

While they play at chess, Owein is discomfited because Athur's men are attacking his 'ravens', until Owein's 'ravens' turn the tables on Arthur's troops, "carrying the men up into the air and pulling them apart and letting the pieces fall to the ground." 'Alba of the ravens' might suggest a land of bloodthirsty and superstitious 'painted' or 'tattooed' warriors: the Picts.

If Columba had come to stamp out paganism and to spread the Word of God, he and his fellows must have resembled Druids themselves. In contrast to the Roman tonsure of St Peter, the Celtic monks favoured a frontal tonsure: the fronts of their heads were shaved bare, while their hair flowed long behind. Their eyelids were stained or painted, and they spoke a 'strange language' amongst themselves, reverting to Latin when relevant. They wore homespun garments and carried a staff or 'bachall'.

They built their refectory around the Moel-blàtha, the 'flat stone of division', a granite boulder deposited during the Ice Age near **Cladh an Diseirt**, the 'Burial Ground of the Hermitage'. "Luck," we are told, "was left on all the food that was put on the flat stone of division." Their simple huts of sticks and turf were arranged around a central space. In addition to industry – the community must have included a smith and a carpenter, and clothing and footwear had to be made – agriculture would have kept the monks employed.

Adomnán recounts a story of the monks returning to their huts across the island after a hard day's work in the fields. Coming up Gleann Cùlbhuirg – the 'Glen at the Back of the Fort', otherwise known as **Gleann Teampuill**, the 'Glen of the Temple'

– the monks reached the halfway point. Here they experienced "a wonderful fragrance like all flowers gathered into one; and of heat like fire, not the fire of torment but somehow sweet." Lightness and joy filled them, easing the remainder of their journey. The cause was the ageing Columba, sending out his spirit to refresh the brethren.

The community – Columba's 'Family' – grew, swelled by Irish, British, Pictish and Saxon pilgrims and penitents. An old Irish verse remarks:

> "Wondrous the warriors who abode in Hi,
> Thrice fifty in the monastic rule,
> With their boats along the main sea,
> Three score men a-rowing."

The end came for Columba in 597. On the thirtieth anniversary of his arrival, he had seen angels standing on a rock across the Sound – "It is as though they wish to draw near me to call me from the body but they are not allowed to come any closer and they will soon hasten back to the heights of heaven." He gave himself another four years, holding on through that final Easter so as not to turn the festival of gladness into one of sorrow for his monks. On a Sunday in May he had seen an angel flying over him as mass was celebrated. "How wonderful and without compare is the fineness of an angel's nature," he said.

On a Sabbath day shortly afterwards, Columba blessed the heaps of grain in the community's barn, and confided in his servant that "At midnight this Sunday, as Scripture saith, 'I shall go the way of my fathers.' For now my Lord Jesus Christ deigns to invite me, and I shall go to him when he calls me in the middle of the night." A faithful white horse approached Columba, pressing its head against his chest. Columba blessed the horse, then climbed the hillock which overlooked his monastery and blessed the island. He returned to his hut, where he was writing out a copy of the psalms, but laid off after he had written, "The young lions do lack and suffer hunger: but they that seek the Lord shall not want any good thing." (Psalm 34, verse 10.) Resting on his bed of bare rock and his stone pillow, he gave his last instructions to the brethren: "Love one another unfeignedly. Peace."

As the monastery bell rang out the midnight hour, Columba ran ahead of his monks into the church. His servant following saw the church filled with the radiance of angelic light, and found the saint lying before the altar. He had just strength enough to move his hand in blessing. It was the 9th June, 597.

Lugaid mac Tailchain, in a monastery far away, told his brother at dawn: "During this night just past, St Columba, the pillar of many churches, passed to the Lord. And in the hour of his blessed going, I saw his island of Iona. Though I have never been there in the flesh, yet in the Spirit I could see it, bathed in the bright light of angels. And all the air and sky above even to the heavenly ether was filled with the radiance of the countless angels sent down from heaven to carry home his soul."

Altus Prosator

"He went with two songs to heaven after his cross"
(Dallán Forgaill: 'Amra Choluimb Chille')

Of the poems attributed to Columba, the most magnificent is his 'Altus Prosator', a depiction of the Creation, Fall and Judgement in rhymed Latin. The stanzas start with the letters of the alphabet in sequence, so that the first stanza begins with the word 'Altus', the second with 'Bonos', the third with 'Caeli', etc.

Altus prosator vetustus dierum et ingenitus
erat absque origine primordii et crepidine ...

"**A**ll-High Creator, first-rendered, most ancient and
un-engendered,
who was the true original, un-ageing and primordial,
is and will for eternity extend unto infinity,
to whom Christ his son surrendered, and the Holy Spirit tendered,
co-existing, the Trinity, in glorious divinity,
not to three gods are we sundered, for by us one God is
numbered,
who saves our faith in three splendid persons in great glory
blended."

In Stanza 'B', Columba describes the creation of the angels and archangels, the Principalities and Powers, and in Stanza 'C', the fall of Lucifer and the apostate angels. Stanza 'D' describes the 'great Dragon' – the serpent – dragging a third of the stars down with him into the pit. The stanza beginning 'Excelsus mundi' has the Lord planning and making the heavens and the earth, the waters, trees, sun, moon, stars, birds, fish, cattle, and finally man. In Stanza 'F', the angels sing praises and give thanks to the Creator 'out of love and choice'.

A second Fall comes in Stanza 'G', the devil having tested the 'first two parents'. Stanza 'H' – Hic sublatus – depicts a world inhabited by evil spirits:

> "He was ejected from the horde and subjected by our true Lord;
> the very air is a morass crammed with a most unholy mass
> of spectres light and nebulous, duplicitous, nefarious,
> who, by their wicked example and their behaviour criminal,
> no fence or wall impregnable to hide the abominable,
> would tempt us to a sinful fall before the very eyes of all."

Stanza 'I' discusses the action of water, from the ocean, into refreshing rain, back into the earth, and returning to the sea. In Stanza 'K', Columba reminds us that God has the power to cast down kings and giants, and Stanza 'L' notes the Lord's economy with the waters, regulating clouds and rivers.

Stanza 'M' is concerned with hell, or Gehenna, and Stanza 'O' examines the plight of those who were essentially holy but were unable to open the Book of the Lord, and must therefore await the coming of Christ.

Stanza 'P' describes Paradise, planted by the Lord in the beginning, complete with its fountain and the Tree of Life. Stanza 'Q' concerns Moses, the judge of the Israeli people: "Who, under the Lord's watchful eye, did venture up Mount Sinai?"

From Stanza 'R' to the end, the burden of the poem is Columba's Dies Irae. The Lord's Day is at hand, a day of anger and distress. The love of women will cease, as will the striving of men in this world. Stanza 'S' sees us standing before the seat of judgement, trembling, sobbing, as our crimes are read out to us. In Stanza 'T', the first archangels blow their trumpet, bursting open the graves and tombs.

Stanza 'U' – Vagatur ex climactere – demonstrates Columba's interest in star-gazing:

> "**V**eering from his apogee, Orion moves erratically,
> the Pleiades remaining thus, of all the stars most marvellous,
> from changing Thetis of the sea, whose east is yet a mystery,
> on his settled axis turning, to his certain path returning,
> after two full years have gone by, Vesper comes to the evening sky–
> These symbols are, to the discerning, signs – not articles of learning."

Vesper – the evening star – here symbolizes Christ. In Stanza 'X', Christ descends from the heavens, bringing fire to the world. Stanza 'Y' depicts thousands of angels rejoicing, the elders bowing before the Lamb of God, and the Holy Trinity praised for all eternity.

> "**Z**ealously will the fire dispose of adversaries such as those
> who do deny that Christ the Lamb from God the Father surely came,
> but straight to heaven we shall fly to meet him at his throne on high,
> and so shall we accompany our Lord in ranks of dignity
> according to our proper merit, eternity we shall inherit,
> abiding glory will be on us from aeon unto aeon."

These twenty-four stanzas neatly encapsulate the Genesis and Revelation. We can imagine the abbot reading or reciting them to the brothers at their meals, as they were supposedly read to Pope Gregory in Rome.

Politician, missionary and 'island soldier', Columba was a poet on the isle of poetry – and so for centuries the Gael would pray:

> The tongue of Columba in my head,
> The eloquence of Columba in my speech.

Adomnán

On his death in 597, Columba was succeeded by his cousin, Baithéne, who died in 600. He was followed by Lasrén mac Feradaig, another relative of Columba's.

Fergnae, the fourth abbot, appears to have been part-British, and is mentioned by Adomnán as a "young man of natural goodness" who saw the church brightened with angelic light when Columba entered it one winter's night. Fergnae died in 623, to be succeeded by Lasrén's nephew, Ségéne. During the early part of Ségéne's thirty year abbacy, the 'great dispute' erupted. This concerned the difference in methods used by the Roman and Celtic churches in calculating the date of Easter. St Augustine, who arrived in Britain in the year of Columba's death, was on a mission from Pope Gregory the Great to 'romanize' the Celtic churches. This meant forcing them to adopt the Roman tonsure and the Roman dating of Easter. It was Ségéne who sent a monk by the name of Áedán to King Oswald of Northumbria, who had been baptized in exile on Iona. Adomnán reports that Oswald experienced a vision of St Columba the night before his battle against the British king Cadwallon.

Áedán – otherwise known as St Aidan – established a monastery on the holy isle of Lindisfarne, off the Northumbrian coast. Aidan died on the 31st August 651, but the centre he founded was to be a haven of Celtic Christian culture and learning for over two hundred years. The Lindisfarne Gospels stand with the Book of Kells as the finest examples of illuminated manuscripts from the period.

Lindisfarne was first attacked by Vikings in 793 and finally taken eighty years later. A Benedictine priory was founded there in 1083, the ruins of which remain.

Ségéne also began the task of collecting stories and testimonials concerning Columba. After his death on the 12th August 652, the abbacy passed to one Suibne moccu Urthrí, who died in January 657, to be succeeded by Cumméne, who wrote a book on 'the miraculous powers of St Columba' from the stories garnered by his uncle Ségéne.

In Cumméne's time, the Easter dispute broke out again. Bishop Fínán, who had been sent from Iona to continue the work of Aidan on Lindisfarne, had argued with "the most zealous champion of the true Easter": Rónán. King Oswiu of Northumbria observed the Irish Easter. His Kentish queen, however, observed the Roman one, and brought to the Synod of Whitby in 664 an English abbot and a Frankish bishop who succeeded in convincing Oswiu that the authority of St Peter exceeded that of St Columba.

Cumméne died on the 24th February 669, and was succeeded by Failbe, who was abbot of Iona for ten years. On his death, the abbacy passed to Adomnán mac Rónán, who was descended from Columba's grandfather.

Adomnán's death was entered for the 23rd September 704, when he was supposedly in his seventy-seventh year. In the 'Life of Adomnán', written at Kells in the tenth-century, we read his verse:

"If on Iona I should die,
it would be a fair goodbye.
Beneath the azure sky know I
no better spot wherein to lie."

He was friends with King Aldfrith of Northumbria, half-brother to Ecgfrith who was buried on Iona in 685, and used this friendship to negotiate the release of sixty Irish prisoners. He made two visits to Northumbria, and during one he took with him his book, 'The Holy Places'.

Adomnán wrote 'The Holy Places' while "daily beset by laborious and almost insupportable business from every quarter". He seems to have found relaxation in the company of the Frankish bishop Arculf, who visited Iona bringing stories of his travels in the Holy Land. Adomnán grasped the opportunity to write down Arculf's descriptions of Jerusalem and Alexandria, Rome and Constantinople. Bede, who admired Adomnán's book, rewrote in his own less 'intricate' style, and tells us that Aldfrith sent Adomnán "back to his own land richer by many gifts".

The Vita Columbae, or 'Life of St Columba', may have been written by Adomnán "in response to the entreaties of the brethren" to commemorate the centenary of Columba's death. The 'Life' contains three 'books', the first "concerning prophetic revelations", the second book "dealing with miracles of power", and Book Three, "concerning visions of angels".

Adomnán's other historical achievement is recorded in the annals for the year 697: 'Adomnán went to Ireland and gave the Law of Innocents to the peoples.' This Cáin Adomnáin, which was designed to protect churches, children, and especially women from combat, was introduced by Adomnán at an assembly held at Birr. Forty clergymen and fifty kings of Ireland and Scotland stood as its guarantors.

In the second book of his 'Life of St Columba', Adomnán refers to the occasion when the future saint was studying under the bard Gemmán. A cruel man was chasing a young girl, who ran to Columba for protection, but her persecutor drove his spear into her, even as she clutched at the cleric's garments. Columba declared that, "In the same hour in which the soul of the girl he killed ascends to heaven, so be it that the soul of her killer shall descend to hell." At which moment, the killer fell dead on the spot.

Professor D. F. Melia, in 'The Irish Saint as Shaman', recounts a tale of Adomnán as a young man with his mother, Ronnat, discovering a large number of dead women at the site of a battle, including a headless mother with an infant child. At Ronnat's request, Adomnán joined the mother's head to her body, bringing her back to life. She turned out to be the wife of the High King, and she laid an injunction on Adomnán that he should neither eat nor drink until he had "freed all the women of the Western world".

In 704, the Roman church celebrated Easter on the 30th March, the Celtic church on the 20th April. Bede tells us that Adomnán had been won round to the Roman calculation – although it wasn't until 716 that the Saxon Ecgberht came to Iona and persuaded the community to "adopt the canonical rite of Easter and the style of tonsure". By then, Adomnán had been dead for twelve years – in the Venerable Bede's words:

"God in his goodness decreed that so great a champion of peace and unity should be received into everlasting life before he should be obliged, when Eastertide returned once more, to enter upon more serious controversy with those who refused to follow him in the truth."

The White Strand of the Monks

Leaving the abbey grounds, with the Iona Community Shop opposite, we now take the road to the north of the island. Passing through the northern extent of the vallum, we approach Clachanach ('Place of Stones') on the left-hand side. The Duke of Argyll's memorial cross stands to the right of the road, and here the road runs alongside **Iomaire nan Achd**, the 'Ridge of the Acts'.

In 1609, King James VI of Scotland (James I of England) resolved to bring the Highland clans into line. The Bishop of the Isles, Andrew Knox, summoned the Highland chieftains on board a galleon off the shore of Mull on the pretext of hearing a sermon. They were taken hostage and only released on condition that they attended a conference on Iona.

In July of 1609, the chiefs of the Highland clans signed up to a code of nine statutes – the Statutes of Iona. Although it would be a good fifty years before the clans began to implement the acts, they did represent a new understanding between the clans and the monarchy and were designed to bring order to the Highlands and Islands.

Among other things, the statutes declared that inns were to be established throughout the Highlands and Islands to relieve the poor of the burden of providing hospitality. The practice of 'sorning' – war-bands helping themselves to food and other requirements as they wished – was outlawed, as was the importation of wine, the use of firearms and the bardic art of glorifying warfare. Highland chiefs were to have their sons educated in Lowland schools and were to keep smaller houses to avoid heavy taxation of their people.

The statutes were fiercely anti-Gaelic, as King James detested the "Irish language" and intended to have it abolished. Yet, for all their English bias, the statutes did not prevent the Highlanders from passionately supporting the Stuart cause through the rebellions of the eighteenth century. The 'Ridge of the Acts' commemorates the new pact between the crown and the chiefs, ratified on Iona.

Continuing north, past **Cnoc Cùil Phail**, the 'Hill of Paul's Nook' on the right, the road ends at a gateway opening onto a pasture meadow. A track leads off to the left towards Lagandòrain, 'Little Hollow of the Otter', and the footpath through the gate winds across the sward of Cnoc an t-Suidhe. Running like a white hem from Carraig Àrd Ànnraidh – 'Rock of (the) Height of Storm' – down to Port na Frainge – 'Port of the Frenchman' – is the half-mile of sandy beach known as **Tràigh Bàn nam Manach**, the 'White Strand of the Monks'.

On Christmas Eve, in the year 986, the abbot and fifteen monks were slaughtered on this beach by Viking raiders. For two hundred years they had harried the island, destroying the abbey in 795 and again in 802, murdering sixty-eight monks on the beach of Martyr's Bay in 806, and in 825 storming the church and killing Blathmac mac Flainn for refusing to disclose the whereabouts of St Columba's reliquary.

Much that was precious – including the reliquary and the Books of Kells – was taken to Ireland for safety, yet the church at Iona was rebuilt, time and again, until even the Vikings were converted to Christianity and took to burying their dead in the sacred soil. A runic inscription on a stone from the Reilig Odhráin reads: Kali the son of Ólvir laid this stone over his brother Fugl. Magnus Barelegs refused to sack the church in 1098, and Somerled eventually commissioned the rebuilding of St Oran's Chapel.

Throughout this period, the flame of Celtic Christianity was kept alive by the céli Dé, 'Companions of God'. These often lonely, isolated 'Culdees' took to the barren, inaccessible places, suffering for their communities and for the Lord. While the church of Iona had bowed to Rome – and would in time be destroyed by the Reformation for its Roman practices – the Culdees remained true to the old ideals.

The ghosts of the monks and their Viking harassers are still seen on Iona. One sighting described fourteen longboats appearing from the far side of Eilean Ànnraidh north of the White Strand, the raiders falling on the monks on the shore ...

The island has weathered much in the cause of faith. Pict and Viking, Saxon, Scot and Briton lie buried in its earth; ghosts and angels attest to its spiritual history.

Preparing Vellum

Valiant Michael of the white steeds,
Who subdued the Dragon of blood,
For love of God, for pains of Mary's Son,
Spread thy wing over us, shield us all,
Spread thy wing over us, shield us all.

Mary beloved! Mother of the White Lamb,
Shield, oh shield us, pure Virgin of nobleness,
And Bride the beauteous, shepherdess of the flocks,
Safeguard our cattle, surround us together,
Safeguard our cattle, surround us together.

And Columba, beneficent, benign,
In name of Father, and of Son, and of Spirit Holy,
Through the Three-in-One, through the Trinity,
Encompass thou ourselves, shield our procession,
Encompass thou ourselves, shield our procession.

('Hymn of the Procession': Carmina Gadelica)

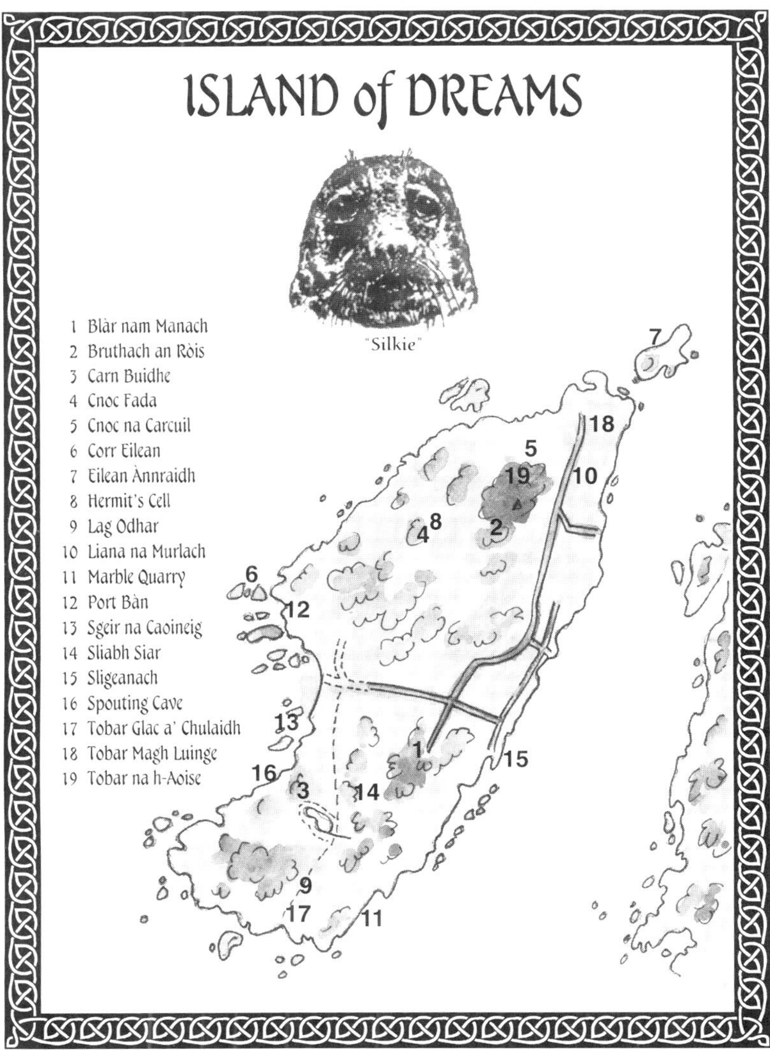
ISLAND of DREAMS
"Silkie"
1 Blàr nam Manach
2 Bruthach an Ròis
3 Carn Buidhe
4 Cnoc Fada
5 Cnoc na Carcuil
6 Corr Eilean
7 Eilean Ànnraidh
8 Hermit's Cell
9 Lag Odhar
10 Liana na Murlach
11 Marble Quarry
12 Port Bàn
13 Sgeir na Caoineig
14 Sliabh Siar
15 Sligeanach
16 Spouting Cave
17 Tobar Glac a' Chulaidh
18 Tobar Magh Luinge
19 Tobar na h-Aoise

IONA

Island of Dreams

Island of Dreams

O angel-haunted Isle where Colum trod,
Fair be thy dreams.
(Bessie J.B. MacArthur)

Iona's two thousand acres play host to many thousands of visitors each year. Some step off the ferry for little more than a couple of hours, walking to Columba's abbey and back before returning to their coaches on Mull. Others come for weeks to live and pray with the Iona Community. From across the world they come to work in the bar and the hotels. While the earnest pursuits of fishing and farming continue, the hundred or so inhabitants of the isle rely on the influx of tourists who from spring to autumn turn the island's single road into a busy thoroughfare.

Life on Iona is not without its struggle. A boating accident in December 1998 took the lives of four young men from the island. The Iona Primary School seldom manages an intake of more than ten, and the children of the island go to high school on the mainland, boarding during the week. There is a small surgery on the island, next door to the school, but emergencies are evacuated by helicopter to Glasgow, where the children of Iona are usually born, a good hundred miles away.

In the winter months, rough weather can seal off the island completely, and this in the days of a modern ferry service. How much more treacherous might the seas have been to men in light coracles? The "shipwreck of a boat of the community of Iona" is recorded in 641, and fifty years later "a gale caused six men of the community of Iona to drown". The year 749 saw "the drowning of the community of Iona". The sea was their livelihood. They hunted seals for meat, skins and oil. Seals are often seen in the seas around Iona and particularly around Fionnphort, where the fishing catch is landed. It is not unusual to see a pod of dolphins making its way along the Sound, an occasion which brings the islanders out in awe, for what a joy it is to have whales and dolphins, seals and otters as your neighbours, rather than as captives in a marine zoo.

Fiona Macleod's tale of Manannan and 'Sunshine', whom the god of the sea brought to his fort on Iona at the time of his Michaelmas festival, preserves the ancient Hebridean legend of the Selchie, or Silkie. 'Sunshine' pined for her sunny lands, till Manannan told her: "You shall be a sleeping woman by day, and sleep in my dún here on Iona: and by night, when the dews fall, you shall be a seal, and shall hear me calling to you from a wave, and shall come out and meet me."

The legends of the Silkie tell of the beautiful children of the King of Lochlann, condemned by their step-mother to live their lives as seals, but for three occasions in the year when the Full Moon is at its brightest. Then the seal-children haul themselves onto the rocks, shed their skins, and dance as humans in the light of the moon till the hour comes for them to slip back inside their skins and take to the waves once more. If one could but steal the skin of a Silkie and hide it away, the poor creature would be unable to return to the sea; many's the story of a fisherman gaining himself a seal-wife by this method, until the Silkie finds her skin again and vanishes into the ocean.

Hó i hó i hi o hó i
Hó i hi o hó ìì
Hó i hó i hi o hó i
Last night I was not alone ...

I am the daughter of Aoid son of Eóghan,
And I know well the skerries.
Woe betide him who would strike me,
For I am a woman of another land.
(From The Songs of John Mac-Codrum)

Seals, with their large round eyes and sleek, dog-like heads, have a habit when they are 'bottling' of observing human beings.

Their plaintive cries and maternal instincts, combined with their competition with fishermen for fish, have created a lore over the years in which some people have the sea in their blood and are part seals themselves. 'The Seal-Woman's Croon', collected in Songs of the Hebrides by Kenneth MacLeod, contains the line, 'An cadal trom 's an deachaidh mi': 'The deep sleep I went into'. As with everything of the sídhe, or faery, these magical seals represent the souls of the departed, as if those whom the sea claims live on in the guise of a seal.

Marjorie Kennedy-Fraser, who lies buried in Reilig Odhráin, sang 'The Seal-woman's Sea-Joy' to a party of seals off Barra:

Ionn da, ionn do,
Ionn da, odar da.
Hiodan dao odar da.
Hiodan dao odar da ...

Uncannily, the seals sang back, "a perfect fusillade of single answering tones", until, in a moment of silence, "a beautiful solo voice" sang. "The voice was quite human in character but much greater in volume than any mezzo-soprano I have ever heard ... In their answering phrase the solo seal sang the interval of an ascending sixth, a favourite melodic step with the Isles folk in their tunes. Did the Isles folk borrow this of the seals or the seals of the Isles folk?"

An Baile Mór

The Big Town faces Fionnphort across the Sound. Visiting the isle in 1810, Sir Walter Scott counted "forty cottages in front of the Nunnery". Around the turn of the twentieth century, these thatched cottages were replaced by two-storey stone buildings with names like Lovedale Cottage, Oran Cottage, and Mo Dhachaidh: 'My Home'. It is an unfortunate habit of tourists to peer in through these windows, neglecting the fact that they are people's dwellings.

"Iona," wrote Scott in a letter of July 29, 1810, "is a very singular place – the remains of the Church though not beautiful are very curious and nothing can be more wonderful than to see the numbers of sculptured monuments of priests and warriors in a place so extremely desolate and miserable. The inhabitants are in the last state of poverty and wretchedness." The population of the island was somewhat larger than it is today: in 1835 no less than 521 people were registered as living on Iona.

James Boswell and Dr Samuel Johnson stayed at Iona Cottage, which looks down on the jetty from the hillside near the fire station, during their Tour of the Hebrides in 1773. They reported mixed feelings:

"We were both disappointed, when we were shown what were called the monuments of the kings of Scotland, Ireland and Denmark, and of a King of France. There are only some grave-stones flat on the earth, and we could see no inscriptions. How far short was this of marble monuments, like those in Westminster Abbey, which I had imagined here!"

On the other hand, Boswell quotes Dr Johnson's words:

"We were now treading that illustrious Island, which was once the luminary of the Caledonian regions, whence savage clans and roving barbarians derived the benefits of knowledge, and the blessings of religion ... Whatever withdraws us from the power of our senses, whatever makes the past, the distant, or the future, predominate over the present, advances us in the dignity of thinking beings ... That man is little to be envied, whose patriotism would not gain force upon the plain of Marathon, or whose piety would not grow warmer among the ruins of Iona."

Felix Mendelssohn also visited, writing in 1829 that, "when in some future time I shall sit in a madly crowded assembly with music and dancing round me, and the wish arises to retire into the loneliest loneliness, I shall think of Iona". He also noted that, "Opposite Iona stands a rocky island which, to complete the effect, looks like a ruined city." When asked by his sisters to describe the Hebrides, Mendelssohn sat down at the piano and picked out the tune that was to become his Hebridean Overture, known as 'Fingal's Cave' from the basalt rock formations of Staffa.

The name 'Fingal's Cave' derives from the poetry of James Macpherson. His 'Fragments of Ancient Poetry Collected in the Highlands of Scotland and Translated from the Gallic or Erse Language' was published in 1760 and triggered the Romantic rediscovery of the Highlands. He attributed his 'fragments' to Ossian, or Oisin, "Little Fawn", the Celtic bard, son of Finn MacCool. Oisin was loved by Niamh of the Golden Hair, daughter of the sea-god Manannan Mac Lir, who took him away to the Land of Promise. In time, Oisin pined for his native land, but on returning he found Ireland a weary, careworn place, and himself a blind and withered old man.

No matter that much of 'Ossian's' work was a forgery; Macpherson single-handedly inspired the Victorian obsession with the Highlands and the subsequent tourist boom. Boats sail from Fionnphort and Am Baile Mór to see the cliffs of Staffa ('Island of Staves'), formed from molten lava, and the colonies of sea-birds that thrive there.

"Many a mortal of these days,
Dares to pass our sacred ways,
Dares to touch audaciously
This Cathedral of the Sea!"
(From 'On Visiting Staffa' by John Keats)

It is interesting to note that the columnar basalt of Staffa, Ulva and Carsaig on Mull find their Irish counterpart at the Giant's Causeway in County Antrim, created – so the legends say – by Finn MacCool to connect him to his lover on Staffa. The 'highway' between Northern Ireland and Western Scotland, so vital to the history of Argyll, was constructed by volcanic activity in the early Tertiary period.

Robert Louis Stevenson visited the cave on Staffa in August, 1870. Later, he dined with friends at the Argyll Hotel, nestled between the cottages of the sea-front. His description of the meal makes lively reading. They waited nearly an hour for their 'nice broth' to arrive. It turned out to be, "purely and simply, rice and water. After this, we have another weary pause, and then herrings in a state of mash and potatoes like iron." Stevenson "dined off broken herring and dry bread", and then came a "fowl in a lordly dish". "'That fowl,' says Bough to the landlady, 'is of a breed I know. I knew the cut of its jib whenever it was put down. That was the grandmother of the cock that frightened Peter.' ... 'Na-na, it's no' so old,' says the landlady, 'but it eats hard.'

Suffice it to say that the reputation of the Argyll Hotel, which opened its doors in 1867, has improved immeasurably.

Stevenson was staying for three weeks at Erraid, on the southern tip of the Ross of Mull, while studying at Edinburgh University. Later he wrote his thrilling adventure 'Kidnapped', in which young David Balfour is shipwrecked off Erraid:

"By this time, now and then sheering to one side or the other to avoid a reef, but still hugging the wind and the land, we had got round Iona and begun to come alongside Mull. The tide at the tail of the land ran very strong, and threw the brig about ... I was on my feet in a minute. The reef on which we had struck was close in under the south-west end of Mull, off a little isle they call Erraid ..."

Balfour finds himself washed up and alone on the tidal islet. "But the creek, or strait, that cut off the isle from the main land of the Ross opened out on the north into a bay, and the bay again opened into the Sound of Iona ... Now, from a little up the hillside over the bay, I could catch sight of the great, ancient church and the roofs of the people's houses in Iona ... It still rained, and I turned in to sleep, as wet as ever, and with a cruel sore throat, but a little comforted, perhaps, by having said goodnight to my next neighbours, the people of Iona."

The Marble Quarry

Travel south out of am Baile Mór, past the shop and the restaurant by Martyr's Bay, and take the road that runs along the sea front, seldom more than a few feet from the rocks and the sand, to where the road turns westwards at **Sligeanach**, a name denoting 'Shelly Ground'. Follow the road past Cnoc an Tobair – the 'Hill of the Well' – and up the Bruthach na Ceapaich, 'Ascent of the Tillage Plot', until a rough track leads off to the left, up past Ruanaich, usually translated as 'Place of Red Flowers' (ruanach: 'firm, steadfast'). Take this track up to the gate that leads into Bealach nan Tuilmean – 'Pass of the Little Knolls' – between Tòn a' Mhanaich and Maol nam Manach – the 'Monk's Bottom' (tòn: 'anus') and the 'Headland of the Monks' (maol: 'tonsured'). We are now crossing the highlands of the south – the **Blàr nam Manach**, the 'Plain (or Battlefield) of the Monks' and the **Sliabh Siar**, the Westward Heath, translated by Fiona Macleod as the 'Hill of Noises'. We are far from the world of am Baile Mór, here – far from anything – and the mind can wander. Does Blàr nam Manach commemorate a battle between Columba's monks and the Pictish Druids who had settled on Iona around 560, or the encounter between Columba and the two 'bishops', identified by the saint as Druids in disguise? For Columba landed at Port a' Churaich, on the southern coast, and not at any of the eastern bays closer to the abbey lands. Might that not indicate that the island was already occupied, possibly by a hostile element Columba was committed to root out? Adomnán does, after all, refer to Columba as an 'island soldier'.

Heading south, we pass through Na h-Àbhain – the 'Hollows', or the 'River' – and on, rounding Cnoc Loisgte ('Burnt Hill') beneath the Big Hill of the Strangers, to come to the House of the Lowlanders, the Big Fairy Mound of the Aird, and down to the Marble Quarry.

Iona's Lewisian marble exists in a vertical band, about twenty feet thick at the sea end, and is composed of white calcerous portions streaked with green serpentine. Other forms of marble can be found near Sloc Dún Mhanannain on the north-west coast, and at Silver Rock near the 'Port of the Dead Man'.

Sacheverell, Governor of the Isle of Man, noted in 1688 that a great 6ft by 4ft block of Iona marble served as the altar in the church, till sightseers and superstitious fisherman removed it piecemeal – Iona Marble is rumoured to be extremely 'lucky' and has the power to avert shipwreck. We can trace quarrying activity on Iona back to 1693, and commercial quarrying flourished in the late eighteenth century. In a rare outreak of industrial heritage on the island, a gas engine and cutting machine, dating from 1907 to 1914, can be found at the quarry, which is classed as a scheduled ancient monument. The visitor might care to seek out the carving of a helmeted warrior, similar to the carved monuments at the abbey, etched into the marble by an unknown hand.

The famed 'Iona Pebble' can be found on most of the southern and western beaches and especially around St Columba's Bay. Thrown up by the action of the waves, these green stones are also locally known as 'Mermaid's Tears'. Small stones of Iona Marble, often carved with crosses, can easily be purchased on the island. According to Adomnán, Columba used a 'white' stone to heal Broichan, Druid to the king of the Picts.

There is some evidence that 'The Three Black Stones' was a Druidic test: three stones – one white, one black, and one speckled – were placed in a bucket full of black water from a bog. If the accused picked out the white stone, they were innocent; if the black one, they were guilty. The speckled stone indicated 'not proven'. Port Chlacha Geal, 'Port of the White Stones', lies at the south end of the Bay at the Back of the Ocean. Port Chlacha Dubh, 'Port of the Black Stones', lies further north, near Calva.

The Spouting Cave

Heading back inland from the Marble Quarry, along the Liana an Tairbh, or 'Meadow of the Bull', we come to Gàradh Eachainn Òig, 'Young Hector's Garden, or Yard'. To turn left here would lead us to **Lag Odhar**, the 'Dappled Hollow', and thence to Port a'

Churaich. Cairns stand above the sea-ground stones of St Columba Bay: thought by some to have been raised by penitent monks or pilgrims, what they truly represent or commemorate is hard to say.

On the slope above Port a' Churaich stood a small village, where news of the Battle of Waterloo was first heard in the region. To the west of the remains of various dwellings, including John MacLean's House at the northern end of Lag Odhar, is Coire Sianta, the intriguingly named 'Charmed, or Sacred, Hollow'. A westward plain leads past Cnoc a' Bhodaich – the 'Old Man's Hill' – towards the 'Port of the Big Mouth'.

Taking the northern track from Lag Odhar, over Staoneig, the walker reaches peaty Loch Staoneig, the island's principal water supply. Turning westwards around **Carn Buidhe**, the 'Yellow Rocky Hill', we come to the western coast of Iona. A plume of sea-spray shoots over the rocks from Uamh an t-Seididh, the 'Cave of the Blowing', otherwise known as the Spouting Cave.

The south-west facing coast of Iona is riven with caves: St Martin's Caves, the Cormorant's Cave, Cave of the Old Man and the Cave of the Little Crosses all join the Spouting Cave on this shore.

We remember the story, told to Fiona Macleod by a man of Tiree, that Mary Magdalene lies buried in a cave on Iona. The tale goes that the Magdalene wandered the world with a blind man, who loved her, though they did not sleep together. She came to Knoidart, in Argyll, where her first husband caught up with her. Fearing for the blind man's safety, she begged him to lie down among some pigs, which she then tended. Her first husband laughed – "That is a fine boar you have there!" – and thrust his spear into the blind man. Then he sheared off the Magdalene's beautiful hair and left her. She died, weeping, and was discovered by a monk of Columba who carried her to Iona, where she was buried.

If we accept, as some scholars insist, that 'Magdalene' was the title of a priestess dedicated to the goddess of the moon, much as 'Brigid' was, then the story begins to make sense. The Magdalene buried in a cave on Iona is the same 'Lady of the

Shores' we have already encountered as Brìde. Brigid – the 'Two-Faced One' – combined the Virgin Mary with her darker half, known to Christianity as the Madgalene.

If we can draw anything from Fiona Macleod's story, it may be that Columba allowed the burial of a Druidic priestess somewhere on the shores of Iona. The blind man who loved her would have been an old Druid or bard, and recalls the pitiful state of Oisin the bard after his sojourn with Niamh of the Golden Hair. Myrddin, in his poem 'Hoianau' ('Greetings'), prophesies to a "little pig" and refers to his beloved sister, a prophetess. Suibhne Geilt, Myrddin's Irish counterpart, suffered a similar fate to that of the 'Magdalene's' companion: speared by a jealous swineherd. At the hill-fort of Dunadd in Kintyre, the capital of Dál Riata, the figure of a boar is carved into a rocky outcrop, besides a carved footprint (where the new king laid his foot) and a fourth century ogham inscription. The tale of the 'Magdalene' recalls the divine priestess or goddess, who tends to the inspired madman who must suffer a ritual death. If further proof were needed, to the north of the Spouting Cave, in Camus Cùl an Taibh stands **Sgeir na Caoineig**, the 'Rock of the Weeper'. Brigid introduced the lament, or 'keening', to Ireland after the death of her son Ruadan at the hands of Goibhniu the smith. Alongside the Weeper's Rock lies Port Ghealtain, the 'Port of the Coward' (gealt: 'madman'). The last vestiges of pagan Druidism can be glimpsed in this tale of the Magdalene and the 'blind man', or rather the priestess and her insane prophet, told by the Tiree man (who has his own rock – Sgeir Fhir Thiridh – just out to sea from the Rock of the Weeper).

Port Bàn

From the Spouting Cave, we return to the path known as Tràill a' Ghairt, a name meaning something like 'drudgery of weeds' and usually translated as the 'Trough of the Cornpatch' – and down the slope to the brilliant pale yellow sands of Camus Cùl an Taibh. This beautiful bay of sand and pebbles stretches for over a kilometre, running north-south along the western flank of the island. It was off this bay that the Guy Mannering sank on the last day of 1865.

A' Mhachair – the low, grassy plain – hugs the bay and was the farmland of Columba's monks. An eighteen hole golf course has been set out on the Machair, teeing off from the end of the island's road, near the Big Fairy Mound, and first heading south towards the hill of Iodhlann Chorrach – 'Steep Cornyard' – and then moving northwards along the western edge of the Machair as far as Cnoc nan Caorach, the 'Hill of the Sheep'.

Beyond the sands of Camus Cùl an Taibh, a series of rocks stretch out into the ocean, from Àrd an Dòbhran – 'Otter's Point' – in the south, to Sgeir Leathan – 'Broad Skerry' – at the northern end of the bay. Between these two lie Port na Cloiche ('Port of the Stone'), Port Ghealtain and the Rock of the Weeper.

At any time of the day, the walk along the Machair, passing Druim na Cruaiche – the 'Ridge of the Heap' – and an Sìthean Mór, where Columba communed with angels – is a peaceful experience of natural wonder. To rest by Camus Cùl an Taibh in the evening, gazing out across the rollers of the Atlantic, is to soak up the extraordinary tranquillity of this sacred isle.

North of the road ending, a stile leads past Cùlbhuirg, the 'Back of the Fort', and Lòn nam Manach, the 'Monks' Marsh (or Food, Provisions)'. The rocky knoll of Eilean a' Chaolais – 'Island of the Strait' – guards Port Pollarain, the 'Port of the Pools', beyond which lies the lovely, sandy bay of **Port Bàn** – 'White Port' – a place popular with the young hotel workers of the island during the long summer evenings, when dusk and dawn mingle.

The Iron Age fort of Dùn-Bhuirg rises to the north-east of Port Bàn, which is flanked by Eilean a' Chlàrsaich, 'Island of the Harp', a place with clear bardic associations. Standing between Harp Island and the sea are **Corr Eilean** and Stac-a'-Chorr, 'Pointed Island' and 'Pointed Stack'. Còrr also means 'crane', a bird of great importance to the Druids because the letters of Ogham, the Celtic script, were formed from the shapes of crane's legs in flight.

In a poem from the Dunaire Fionn, the poet Oisin questions the origins of a 'crane-bag' owned by the sea-god Manannan mac Lir. He is told the story of Aoife, transformed into a crane by a sorceress, who fled to the house of Manannan and lived there for two hundred years. Dùn Mhanannain, 'Manannan's Fort', lies just a short distance along the coast from Port Bàn. Manannan made a bag of her skin which held his sacred treasures, including "The King of Scotland's shears ... and the King of Lochlann's helmet". In another story – Cailleach an Teampuill – Finn MacCool encounters the four death-dealing birds (cranes) known as the 'Children of the Old Woman of the Temple'. Finn saves the four sons by taking three drops of blood from the head of a sacred bull; Tarvortigaranos, or 'Bull with Three Cranes', is the inscription carved on a stone relief in Paris, indicating that cranes and bulls shared a common sacred significance to the Celts.

St Columba kept a pet crane, which he had pluck the eye from a messenger from Finnian who spied on the saint as he completed his copy of the Cathach, or 'battle' psalter. On Iona, he despatched a monk to keep look-out "in the western part of this isle, sitting on the sea-shore" for a crane that had flown towards Iona "from the northern region of Ireland". The exhausted crane spent three days recuperating on the island before taking to the skies and returning to Ireland. Perhaps this story of Columba was designed to deflect the pagan folk interest in sacred cranes and their association with Manannan and his bag of treasures.

The peace of Port Bàn partakes of this Celtic atmosphere of bards and harps, of cranes and mystic Ogham letters, of the sea-god and the poet who dwelt in the Land of Promise. Let the waves wash against the shore, and dream of the bards of old, those shamanic poets rescued from the Hag of the Temple – who was Bride or Brigid in her wintry form – by three drops of blood from the sacred bull.

The Hermit's Cell

Turning inland, a path leads us along the southern edge of Sliabh Meadhonach, the 'Central Moor', and curves round to cross **Cnoc Fada** – 'Long, or Distant, Hill'. We are in the desolate heartlands of Iona, a bewildering landscape of rocky outcrops and marshy ground where the sheep is king. The hill to the south of Cnoc Fada is the Hill of the Brownie, or Monster – uraisg or urraisg: a 'witless savage'. In 'The Supernatural Highlands', Francis Thompson describes the uraisg as a half-man, half-goat creature with long hair, teeth and claws that frequents glens and streams, a tale-teller who scares the traveller with his tales of the three worlds. If the hill in fact commemorates a 'savage', might it not recall a wildman of the Suibhne Geilt or Myrddin Wyllt school, a Druidic bard driven insane and ekeing out an existence at some lonely spot – and if so, where did this poor soul stand in relation to the monks, whose route from the Machair to the church community ran through Gleann Teampuill, south of the Monster's Hill?

Sheltered between Cnoc Fada and Cnoc nam Bradhan Mór, the 'Big Hill of the Querns', nestles the stone remains of Cobhain Cuildich – the 'Coffin of the Culdee' – otherwise known as Cabhan Cùilteach, which has connotations of dark and dismal, a bed or bakehouse, and a skulking female. It is more familiarly known as the 'Hermit's Cell'.

The stones form a near perfect circle, with a south-facing entrance. Adomnán refers to Columba withdrawing from the community to this 'remote hollow' from which he could see the island of Tiree, where several monasteries were sited. The 'Cell' seems a little large for a single hermit's retreat, and we should note the Gaelic meanings of cobhan ('chest', or 'coffin') and cùilteach ('full of ugly nooks', 'a skulking female', 'bed' or 'bakehouse'). It is without doubt a strong possibility that the stone hut was at some point inhabited by a 'culdee' or Christian hermit. The question is: is this the original purpose and meaning of the stone ring? After all, none of the early church structures have survived as they were constructed of wattle and turf.

If we endeavour to translate Cobhan Cùilteach as something like the 'dark coffin of the skulking female' and bear in mind the associations of bed and bakehouse, we begin to perceive a new set of possibilities, one of which would be a structure akin to the Native American sweat-lodge, where heated stones sprinkled with water produced steam in a darkened 'tipi'. The purification of the initiate by steam led to a trance-like state of the vision quest. A short distance to the north of the Hermit's Cell we find

Tobar na Gaoithe Tuath, the 'Well of the North Wind', from which the water might have been taken. A sweat-lodge would account for the 'dark', 'bed', 'bakehouse', 'chest' and 'coffin' connotations, and would suggest strongly a place connected to healing dreams, sacred to the gods of water and the sea. Perhaps here the seer slept on a bull's hide to receive the dream of the royal succession.

If this 'cell' were used for healing, we can compare it to the Asklepion at Epidaurus in Greece where, after a sacrifice, the sufferer was purified in a steam room or bath house before sleeping in an incubation hut. Dogs licked the afflicted body parts, and down on the coast at the northern end of Camus Cùl an Taibh we find Eilean nan Con – 'Island of the Dogs'. If, on the other hand, we refer to the 'skulking female' notion as part of the derivation of Cobhan Cùilteach we are left with the possibility of an oracular priestess or a stone cubicle dedicated to a withdrawn goddess: Brigid of the Mound.

The burial of kings on Iona would suggest that the island was seen as the sacred centre – the Navel or Omphalos – of the Inner Hebrides. Perhaps the most famous Omphalos in the world was at Delphi, where the Pythoness delivered her oracle. This again would relate to Brigid, whose sacred animals were the cow, the raven and the serpent. We know that Brigid's sacred flame was tended in an enclosure through the walls of which no man could peep, and if the priestesses of Brìde originally worshipped on Iona, before their expulsion, might they not have rehoused their temple once a year (at Midsummer), sacrificing one of their number (whose year as the representative of the goddess had come to an end) here at the sacred centre of Iona?

The Irish Omphalos was at Uisnech in County Westmeath. Here, the Druids of Nechtan worshipped until they apparently left Ireland. The legends tell of the beautiful Deirdre 'of the Sorrows' who fled Ireland with her lover, Naoise, and his brothers. They settled in Argyll in the first century after Christ, and a Dùn Mhic Uisneachan, or 'Fort of the Sons of Uisneach', stands at Ledaig just north of the mouth of Loch Etive. Deirdre and the brothers are said to have escaped to an island in the sea before being lured back to Ireland by the duplicitous King Conchobar mac Nessa.

There is some evidence that Deirdre was in fact the daughter of a Pictish king and we know from Queen Medb's encounter with a Druidess in the 'Taín Bó Cúailnge' that the Irish brushed up their magical skills in Scotland:

"Where have you come from?" Medb said.
"From learning verse and vision in Alba," the girl said.

So we might wonder whether the Druidic Sons of Uisneach brought their worship of the god of water and wisdom from the sacred centre of Ireland to the island in the sea that was already a sacred centre of the Picts.

The Hermit's Cell, then, is something like the omphalos of the Island of Dreams, where the seeker came for healing visions, and there can surely be few places in this world more conducive to meditation and the inner quest. To emerge from the lodge, blinking in the clear light of Iona, and to gaze to the west where the Fort of Manannan keeps watch over the vast Atlantic would be like emerging from a steamy chrysalis of lucid dreams into the crystal world of natural wonder.

Although the hill Cnoc nam Bradhan Mór – which stands over Cobhan Cùilteach – is usually translated as the 'Big Hill of the Querns' (i.e. stones for grinding corn), 'bradan' means 'salmon', leading us back to the Salmon of Wisdom from Nechtan's Well. A quern is 'bràth', a feminine noun. The masculine 'bràth' means 'judgement' and 'brath' refers to knowledge, and the pursuit of knowledge. Could it be that the Hermit's Cell truly was the seat of an oracular prophetess? Could this chamber even have been the 'Caer Sidi' or Faery Fortress of Taliesin the bard:

"Perfect is my chair in Caer Sidi:
plague and age hurt him not who's in it –
Manawydan and Pryderi have known it well.
Three organs round a fire sing before it,
and about its points are ocean's streams,
and an abundant well above it
whose liquor is sweeter than white wine."

Dùn Ì

From the Hermit's Cell the path winds east-north-east over Cnoc nam Bradhan Mór and onto the lower flanks of Dùn Ì, the Hill Fort of Iona. Passing to the south of Fang Mhairi, or 'Mary's Enclosure', the route curls round the western side of Dùn Ì then climbs rapidly to the summit – at 101 metres, Iona's highest point.

A vast panorama stretches in all directions, looking north to the isle of Rhum, and Skye beyond, with Fladda and Staffa in between; north-east over Ulva and the north end of Mull; eastwards towards Ben More, Ben Buie and far-off Ben Cruachan; south-east towards Jura, the mountains known as the Paps of Jura, and south towards Islay. Facing westwards, the tiny speck of Skerryvore pokes out from the sea, and to the north-west, Tiree and far-flung Barra, then the Dutchman's Cap and Lunga isles, with Coll in the background and South Uist beyond.

From the cairn at the top of Dùn Ì, Iona lies all around – the low farmlands of Calva to the north, and the white strip of Tràigh-na-Criche – 'Boundary Strand' – and Tràigh an t-Suidhe – the 'Strand of the Seat', better translated as the 'Strand of the Sitting'. Beyond lies Eilean Chalbha, 'Calf Island', and past the headland known as Àrd Ànnraidh lies the charming islet called **Eilean Ànnraidh** – 'Storm Island', from ànradh, meaning 'distress' or 'disaster', perhaps commemorating the longship fleet that emerged from this islet with its picturesque east-facing beach to slaughter the monks on the White Strand. Between Dùn Ì and Lagandòrain stands the curiously named **Cnoc na Carcuil** or 'carcair', the 'Hill of the Prison', recalling the prison of Gwair, mentioned by the bard Taliesin as lying in Caer Sidi, the Faery Fortress. Adomnán records a layman called Guaire mac Áedáin, the "strongest man in the whole of Dalriada", as being told by Columba that the cause of his death would be a "companion ... from whom you suspect nothing". This companion turned out to be a knife that stabbed Guaire in the thigh – recalling a druidic method of blood-letting. The name Guaire mac Áedáin suggests a son of Áedán mac Gabhráin, king of Dál Riata who was crowned by Columba on Iona in 574. Another son of Áedán's was Artuir, otherwise known as Arthur. Taliesin's poem tells of Arthur's expedition to Caer Sidi to release Gwair (Guaire?) from his prison and to capture the Cauldron of Rebirth.

Turning to the east, the view from Dùn Ì looks out over Sloc na Cailleach Oidhche, the 'Gully of the Old Woman of the Night (i.e. the Owl)', and down to the 'French Port' at the southern end of the White Strand of the Monks, beyond the Hill of Paul's Retreat. To the south of this lies **Liana na Murlach**, the 'Meadow of the Fishing-Basket' (or 'Kingfisher)', which was also known as Liana na h-Uilidh, possibly from ulaidh, meaning 'hidden treasure' or 'darling'. What this means is open to question. Was a treasure of some kind deposited in this eastern meadow looking over the Sound of Iona – and if so, what? Some relic of Columba? Or something earlier, perhaps? We are standing on top of the Island of Dreams, so we are allowed to free the imagination and ponder the deeper meaning of Taliesin's poem, the "Spoils of Annwn".

The sixth-century bard Taliesin was attached to the court of Maelgwyn of Gwynedd, who fathered King Bruide, ruler of the Picts in the time of Columba. Taliesin later seems to have served King Urien of North Rheged (Cumbria). Urien brought together the North British Alliance of kings to fight against the Picts and the Saxons. Both Urien and his son Owein fought alongside Artuir, who seems to have married a British woman from the kingdom of Rheged: she is known in the romances as Guinevere, or Gwenhwyfar ('White Spirit') and bears many a similarity to the White Lady, Brigid or Bride. King Rhydderch Hael ('the Generous') of Strathclyde sought Columba's prophecy on his likely manner of death, as we know from Adomnán. So Columba was a contemporary of the kings who fought with Arthur and who feature in the bardic verses of Taliesin.

In later Norman stories of Arthur, the knights of the Round Table are sent in search of the Holy Grail, a vessel related to the Celtic Cauldron and which in some versions is a chalice or cup, associated with Joseph of Arimathea and the Last Supper, and in other versions is a stone – like the fabled Stone of Destiny. The Grail is discovered at the court of the Fisher King, where a king, wounded in the thigh, suffers until the magical question is asked. Traditionally it is Parsifal (from Peredur, joint king of Ebruac –

York – who reigned in the time of Columba) who finds the Grail Castle.

Áedán mac Gabráin earned himself the name 'Pen Vradog', or 'Treacherous King', when he abandoned the British kingdom of Manau Gododdin (roughly, Lothian) to take the crown of Dál Riata. His son Artuir was accepted as a hero by the embattled Britons when he took charge of the defence of Manau Gododdin, probably taking as his headquarters the old Roman fort of Camelon, just north of the Antonine Wall. Adomnán tells us that Artuir fell in battle against the 'Miathi' or Maeatae tribe of southern Picts, near Stirling.

Procopius of Caesarea, writing in the sixth century, claimed that to the Britons the lands north of the Wall were seen as a deadly environment to which the souls of the dead immediately travelled. This would associate Pictland with the Celtic Hades – Annwn – inhabited by the 'Picti' or 'Pritani': the original Britons. When Taliesin wrote of his journey with Arthur to take the Cauldron of the Chief of Annwn, he might be referring to either Áedán, king of Dál Riata, or Bruide, king of the Picts, as the Lord of Annwn.

> "I merit better than the makers of clerkly books
> Who have not seen Arthur's might beyond Caer Wydyr ('Glass Castle')
> Sixth thousand men stood high upon its wall.
> It was difficult to speak with their sentinel ..."

The journey with Arthur is described as a 'splendid labour', a 'sorrowful journey' and a 'lamentable meeting'. Only seven men returned.

The poem tells us of nothing that Arthur does, nothing he says – so that we would be justified in wondering whether the voyagers were accompanying an Arthur who was mortally wounded – if not dead – into the Otherworld. Of Caer Sidi, Taliesin tells us that none before Gwair had been sent into it. If Gwair – or Guaire mac Áedán – had suffered a sacrificial death by means of a wound to the thigh (Adomnán tells us he was sitting under an upturned boat at the time) and had been buried on Iona, then perhaps Taliesin's poem tells us of the journey taking Artuir to the family plot. Given that Columba was uneasy about anointing Áedán king, it would not be unnatural for a son – Guaire – to be given as a hostage to guarantee the king's noble rule. And we should not forget the persistent story of Columba burying Oran.

"The world's wonder: a grave for Arthur," claims an old Welsh tradition, and yet if Artuir died fighting for the Britons of Manau Gododdin, might not his body have been brought to the holy island where his ancestors – the sons of Erc – are said to be buried, and where his father was crowned by St Columba?

The search for the Cauldron of Rebirth connects the quest to the healing properties of water. If we accept that a number of warriors were buried with Artuir ("save seven, none returned") then we might be looking for a burial cist, possibly close to a water source. Two possibilities present themselves, the first lying at the south end of the island: the sixty foot mound attributed to the burial of Columba's coracle, close to **Tobar Glac a' Chulaidh**, the 'Well of the Hollow of the Boat'. A number of cairns stand close by, the meaning of which is unknown. Perhaps the story of Columba's monks burying their curragh above Port a' Churaich was intended to draw attention away from the pagan trappings of Artuir's funeral. After all, Taliesin had no time for the clerics, and no doubt they had little time for him. If Artuir's boat, 'Prydwen', was taking him and his warriors on an Otherworldly journey, was Columba eager not to publicise the fact – especially if the 'layman' Guaire mac Áedán had already preceeded his brother into the Otherworld after a sacrificial rite.

Another possibility directs us towards **Tobar Magh Luinge**, the 'Well of the Plain of the Ship', at the north end of the island. Here we find various humps, including the Hill of the Prison, the Hill of the Field of Tongues (Cnoc an Teanganaich) – which might relate to the ship (luinge or lunga) by way of the Latin 'lingua' and hint at the Gaelic luinneag, a mournful voice or chorus. There is also the Hill of the Height of Storm ('distress', 'disaster' or 'disorder') and the Hill of the Sitting, usually described as the Hill of the Seat, close by Lagandòrain – the 'Little Hollow of the Otter' (dòbhran: 'otter'; dòrainn: 'anguish, lamenting').

There is also, of course, the mysterious Ealadh of Martyr's Bay at the start of the Street of the Dead, and the equally odd Sìthean Mór on the west coast, where twelve bodies were rumoured to lie beneath its long-since vanished circle of stones.

The poem of Arthur's journey to Caer Sidi also tells us:

> "And when we went with Arthur – a sorrowful journey –
> Except seven, none returned from Manawyddan's Caer."

A straight translation of 'Manawyddan's Caer' would be Dùn Mhanannain, on Iona's western coast.

Myrddin was hunted down in his forest hideout by King Rhydderch Hael of Strathclyde, that same Rhydderch who sent a messenger to Columba to enquire as to whether he would die in battle. King Áedán mac Gabráin of Dál Riata appears to have waged war on Rhydderch of Strathclyde, and Myrddin's poem 'Peiryan Vaban' ('Commanding Youth') indicates that Áedán might be attacking Strathclyde in revenge for the slaughter of the pagans at Arderydd in 573. Rhydderch was a Christian, and his appeal to Columba may well have confirmed the saint's worst fears that the king of Dál Riata he crowned on Iona was not wholly committed to the Christian faith (Adomnán records that Columba was visited over three nights by an angel who struck him, insisting that he anoint Áedán king over his preferred choice of Éogenán). The youth 'Mabon' or 'Maban' Myrddin appeals to in his poem is the divine youth rescued from his Otherworldly prison by Arthur in British myth, and who is paralleled by Gwair – or Guaire – in Caer Sidi.

It would only have been true to type if Taliesin had gone insane after his sojourn in Caer Sidi. Perhaps he became the witless savage of Cnoc Urrais, roaming the uplands of Iona and frightening the monks with his tales of the Upper, Lower and Middle Worlds. Perhaps it was he who was sustained by the 'Magdalene' figure, that Mary of Magdala, the 'Village of the Doves'. She appears in the Grail Romances as the Loathly Lady, the 'Black Maiden' (c.f. Brigid) whose garments are embroidered with the grail-symbol of the dove and who is closely connected to the snake-goddess or Pythoness.

The 'Mabon' referred to earlier was the son of 'Modron', the Great Mother. King Urien of North Rheged was supposed to have married one Modron ferch Afallach ('Mother, daughter of Afallach'), and we have already seen how Afallach – or Avalon – might relate to the silver apples of the moon and the priestesses of Brìde. Other traditions have Urien – who was slain in 590 – married to Morgan, Arthur's 'sister'. What is more, she was said to have married King Lot of Lothian, for whom Artuir would have fought in Manau Gododdin. Morgan appears to have held the post of High Priestess, so that her marriage to several kings is actually their 'sacred marriage' to the Goddess of Sovereignty: namely Brigantia. Welsh tradition has it that Modron ferch Afallach was a sister-in-law to King Maelgwyn of Gwynedd – who was both father of Bruide of the Picts and patron to Taliesin before the bard moved north. According to the grail legends it was Morgan who bore Arthur to the isle of Avalon. Was this 'sea-born' Morgan the last priestess of Brìde – the 'Mother' and 'Magdalene' who tended the aged, raving bard after the disaster of the battle at the River Allan, known to the romancers as Camlann?

And the hidden treasure in the Meadow of the Fishing-Basket, or the Kingfisher? How difficult it is not to turn the kingfisher into the Fisher King (the wounded Arthur, or his thigh-pierced brother) in which case what might the darling treasure in the Meadow of the Fishing-Basket be? Could this have been the enamelled, pearl-rimmed Cauldron of the Lord of Annwn, warmed by the breath of nine maidens, which evolved into the Grail of legend – and which was allegedly brought to the west by that Dove-Priestess, Mary of Magdala? Or maybe the oracular Stone of Destiny ... Or could Port nam Murlach refer to the place where the initiate landed, like Taliesin, in a wicker boat known as the crane-bag – in which case the hidden treasure is that for which the island was first renowned: poetic inspiration and the bardic arts of the aois-dàna.

From Dùn Ì, we look down at the ferry crossing from Fionnphort to am Baile Mór and back again, and the abbey – that hive of industry and magnet to tourists and pilgrims the world over – and the sea, sparkling away to the south, and the rough back of Iona.

And so we step a few yards to the northern extremity of Dùn Ì to visit the dark tarn that is **Tobar na h-Aoise**. The Well of Age, or Antiquity. The Well of the People – aois-dàna, the especially gifted. Possibly even Tobar Naoise, the 'Well of Naoise', friend and lover of Deirdre of the Sorrows, who eloped with her to Etive, escaping to an 'island in the sea' when the king of the Picts expressed his desire for the beautiful girl. Naoise and his brothers were the Druids of Nechtan, the 'Sons of Uisneach'. When they left, "all wisdom flowed out of Ireland".

The visitor should wash his or her face in Tobar na h-Aoise, especially at dawn when the first rays of the sun appear, for then the Well of Youth will grant its health and healing, and through its wise waters the dark and ugly cailleach is eternally renewed as the blessed White Lady, Brigid the beautiful.

On the south-eastern slope of Dùn Ì lies **Bruthach an Ròis** – the 'Ascent of the Rose' (ròs: 'a rose', or 'knowledge'). Here the gentle Brìde grew up. Here the bards came for inspiration, the Druids for knowledge. Here Columba walked. Kings were buried and Lords of the Isles anointed. Vikings pillaged. Churches were built, and pilgrims came. Acts were passed. Life was lived. And now a new generation comes to Iona, to gaze at the clear sea water, to top up on tranquillity and spiritual refreshment, and to dream.

May they all climb the Steep Path of Knowledge to the top of the hill and drink from the Well of Antiquity.

"Iona the metropolis of dreams"

- Fiona Macleod

Index

Glossary of place-names on Iona

Allt a' Chaorainn – Brook of the Rowan 46
am Baile Mór – the Big Town 46, 85ff, 103
am Bruthas – the Porridge 17
A' Mhachair – The Machair 24, 93
An Àird – The Height 11
an Ealadh – the Mound (or Tomb) 18, 44, 101
Àrd an Dòbhran – Point of the Otter 93

Bealach nam Ban – Pass of the Woman (or Women) 15
Bealach nan Tuilmean – Pass of the Little Knolls 89
Blàr nam Manach – Plain, or Battlefield, of the Monks 89
Bol Leithne – Eithne's Bowl (or Cattle-fold) 17, 21
Bruthach an Ròis – Ascent of the Rose (or Knowledge) 104
Bruthach na Ceapaich – Ascent of the Tillage-Plot 89
Buaile nan Cailleach – The Old Woman's Cattle-fold 15
Buidhneach – Place of the Yellow Flowers (?):
'numerous' or 'in companies' 60

Cabhan Cùilteach – Hermit's Cell;
('dark bed of the skulking female') 95
Caibeal Muire – Mary's Chapel 55
Camus Cùl an Taibh – Bay at the Back of the Ocean
(or 'the Substance', 'the Vision') 24, 92, 93, 96
Carn Buidhe – Yellow Rocky Hill 91
Carn Cùl ri Eirinn – Cairn of the Back to Ireland 68
Carraig an Daimh – Rock of the Ox (or Oxen) 11
Carraig Àrd Ànnraidh – Rock of the Height of Storm 78
Cill Chainnich – Kenneth's Chapel 19
Cill mo Ghobhannan – Chapel of my Govannon (Goibhniu) 23
Cill mo Neachdain – Chapel of my Nechtan 19, 20, 23, 32
Clachanach – Field of Stones 19, 77
Cladh an Diseirt – Burial-Ground of the Hermitage 69
Cladh na Meirghe – Burial-Ground of the Banner ('signal') 19
Cladh nan Druineach – Burial-Ground of the Craftsman 18
Cnoc a' Bhodaich – Hill of the Old Man 91
Cnoc an Teanganaich – Hill of the Field of Tongues 101
Cnoc an Tobair – Hill of the Well 89
Cnoc an t-Suidhe – Hill of the Sitting (or the Couple) 17, 78
Cnoc Cùil Phail – Hill of Paul's Nook, or Retreat 78
Cnoc Daraich – Oak Hill 46
Cnoc Fada – Long, or Distant, Hill 94, 95
Cnoc Loisgte – Burnt Hill 89
Cnoc Mór – Big Hill 17, 46
Cnoc na Carcuil – Hill of the Prison 98
Cnoc nam Aingeal – Hill of the Angels 24
Cnoc nam Bó – Hill of the Cow 11
Cnoc nam Bradhan Mór – Big Hill of the Querns
('Hill of the Big Salmon'?) 95, 97, 98
Cnoc na Meirghe – Hill of the Banner (or Signal) 19
Cnoc nam Marbh – Hill of the Dead 32
Cnoc nan Caorach – Hill of the Sheep 93

Forthcoming books from Kayelle

"ARTHUR – Lord of Battles"

Man or myth? The greatest hero of the British Isles belonged neither to Cornwall nor Wales. "ARTHUR – Lord of Battles" explores the violent times in which he lived and identifies the 'once and future king' as a genuine Scottish prince who fought alongside thirteen British kings and inspired countless generations.

"Living Scripts"

Easy to use, enjoyable and enlightening, "Living Scripts" is a step-by-step guide to the art of screenwriting for film and television and a revelation of the creative process. Compiled by an award-winning scriptwriter, consultant and tutor, "Living Scripts" will unleash creativity and improve all aspects of the aspiring writer's work.

www.kayelle.co.uk